FOOTSTEPS TO
AmericA

West Indian Americans

by Alexandra Bandon

new
Discovery
B·O·O·K·S
New York

Maxwell Macmillan Canada
Toronto

Maxwell Macmillan International
New York   Oxford   Singapore   Sydney

ACKNOWLEDGMENT

Special thanks to the immigrants who shared their personal stories. Their names have been changed to protect their privacy.

PHOTO CREDITS

front cover: Brian Vaughan; front and back cover (flag photo): Richard Bachmann; The Bettmann Archive: 8, 13, 24, 96; UPI/Bettmann Newsphotos: 20, 62, 67, 70, 98, 101; Mary Ellen Mathews: 32, 37, 44, 56, 75, 77, 82, 85, 89, 103; Alexandra Bandon: 40

New Discovery Books
Macmillan Publishing Company
866 Third Avenue
New York, NY 10022

Maxwell Macmillan Canada Inc.
1200 Eglinton Avenue East
Suite 200
Don Mills, Ontario M3C 3N1

Macmillan Publishing Company is part of the Maxwell Communication Group of Companies.

First edition
Printed in the United States of America

10 9 8 7 6 5 4 3 2 1

LIBRARY OF CONGRESS CATALOGING–IN–PUBLICATION DATA

Bandon, Alexandra
West Indian Americans / by Alexandra Bandon.
p. cm. — (Footsteps to America)
Includes bibliographical references
ISBN 0-02-768148-3
1. West Indian Americans—Juvenile literature. [1. West Indian Americans.] I. Title II. Series.
E184.W54B36 1994   93–27201
973'.04969729—dc20
Summary: A look at West Indian Americans—where they come from, the difficulties they have assimilating in the United States, and how their heritage remains an important part of their new lives. Told with factual information and firsthand oral history accounts.

Contents

Part I

Before the United States

= 1 =

Why Do They Leave?

Colonization and Slavery

The West Indies is a group of English-speaking islands and nations scattered throughout the Caribbean Sea south of the United States. Once known as the British West Indies, these islands and nations are former or current British colonies and current members of the British Commonwealth of Nations. They include Jamaica, the Bahamas, Bermuda, the Leeward Islands (St. Kitts-Nevis, Antigua and Barbuda, Montserrat, Anguilla, and the British Virgin Islands), the Windward Islands (St. Vincent and the Grenadines, St. Lucia, Dominica, and Grenada), the Cayman Islands, Barbados, Trinidad and Tobago, as well as Belize (formerly British Honduras) in Central America, and Guyana (formerly British Guiana) in South America.

West Indian American describes a West Indian who has come to live in America permanently. When West Indians leave their country, they are emigrants and when they get to America, they are immigrants (leaving a country is emigrating; coming to a country is immigrating). The children of West Indian Americans are second-generation West Indian Americans. All West Indian Americans are part of the larger group of Caribbean Americans, which includes Cuban, Haitian, Dominican, and other non-English-speaking immigrants originally from the Caribbean area. The majority of West Indian Americans are black, descendants of the slaves who once lived on the islands.

Christopher Columbus got his first glimpse of the New World in 1492 when he landed in the West Indies, probably in the Bahamas. The West Indies were so named because Columbus assumed he had reached his destination of India. When he arrived, the islands were inhabited by Carib (for whom the Caribbean is named) and Arawak Indians. But years of Spanish colonial rule, which brought disease, war, and slavery to the tribes, virtually killed off the native population.

In the mid-1600s, when the British colonized some of the Caribbean islands and won control of others from a failing Spanish empire, they began importing black slaves from Africa to work the tobacco and sugar plantations. The slaves brought to the West Indies were part of the famous triangle trade: the British exchanged rum for slaves on the west coast of Africa, transported the slaves to the West Indies, where they were taken off the ships and sugar and molasses were taken on, then finally returned to New England, where the sugar and molasses were unloaded to be distilled into rum. After a short "seasoning" period, many of the slaves left in the West Indies were to be sent to the North American colonies, but few actually made the final leg of the trip. It has been estimated that half the slaves taken from Africa for the slave trade went to the West Indies. Only 6 percent went to North America.

Slave society developed in the West Indies between 1640, when Britain first colonized the area, and 1838, when slavery and the resulting apprenticeship in these colonies ended. Plantation owners in the West Indies seldom settled in the

Columbus landing in what is now the Bahamas, where he was met by the Carib and Arawak Indians. His 1492 "discovery" of the New World opened the way for colonization of the Caribbean by Europeans.

islands permanently. They did not bring their families or create a large white majority in the area. Quite the opposite: The West Indian colonies had a black slave majority. Many strong hands were needed to work the sugar crops, and Britain regularly imported as many slaves as were necessary, replenishing a slave population that was exhausted and literally worked to death in the sugar fields. With so few whites and so many blacks on the islands, the white plantation owners gave more responsibilities to their slaves than did their North American counterparts. West Indian slaves were allotted small plots of land for growing fruits and vegetables, which they could then keep for themselves or sell at the local markets.

Emancipation and Emigration

In 1834, Britain abolished slavery, setting aside a period of six years of apprenticeship for former slaves to make the transition into freedom. By the time the apprenticeship period ended in 1838, two years early, the free blacks were quite eager to strike out on their own. They had experience in business from selling the produce they had grown on their allotted land. And because whites were a minority in the West Indies, blacks became craftsmen, such as tailors and blacksmiths, and even professionals, like doctors and lawyers. No lower- or middle-class white society existed on the islands, so blacks had to train for these jobs in order to serve the large black majority.

Not every ex-slave was guaranteed a job, however. Throughout the 19th century, many were forced to migrate (move around) to other islands and countries in search of work.

Though most stayed within the Caribbean, a steady trickle of emigrants headed for the United States. Population levels and economic conditions in most of the West Indian islands were becoming unbearable, and freed slaves looking for work were pushed out of their native areas.

For the first time since slavery began in the area, black women were allowed to raise their own children, and the former slaves began having families. During slavery, the black population had increased more through the importation of additional slaves than through births among the slaves because the hard work on the plantations killed more slaves than were born. In addition, the slave trade had been outlawed in 1807, so no new slaves had been imported from Africa since then. The population of most West Indian colonies fell in the early 19th century. But when slavery ended and families began to form, the population of the islands exploded. Soon there were too many people to be supported by the few jobs available.

To make matters worse, in 1846 Britain passed the Sugar Duties Act, which removed a special protection afforded to West Indian sugar in the English market. The new lower price on sugar caused by the act meant that the planters didn't make as much money and couldn't afford to pay high wages to the people who worked on the plantations. Many plantation workers left the farms in search of more lucrative jobs.

Wages fell even more in the second half of the century when severe hurricanes, widespread drought, and cane disease ruined crops and lost money for many planters. The poverty that resulted from the losses forced many West Indians to find new work or face starvation. Riots brought on by underemployment and overpopulation occurred throughout the Caribbean in the 1860s. By

the 1870s, many island governments were encouraging emigration to avoid food shortages, disease, and political unrest.
Barbados even passed laws in 1873 to help the poor leave.

Unfortunately, wages didn't rise in response to the rioting
or the migration, basically because the plantation owners found
labor willing to work at the lower rates. Many West Indians
refused to take jobs on sugar plantations for the wages the
growers were forced to pay, because the work was difficult, tax-
ing even the strongest field hand. But instead of raising wages
to meet the requirements of the former slaves, the plantation
owners recruited cheap labor, first from India and later from
China. To this day, strong Asian Indian and Chinese influences
remain in West Indian culture.

Native Jamaicans, Trinidadians, Barbadians, and other
West Indians could not compete with the Asian Indian and
Chinese workers who were willing to do difficult work for
extremely low wages. Furthermore, in West Indian society,
sugar cutting on one's own island was considered a low-class
occupation, below the status of most West Indian workers. In a
society very much influenced by class, where occupation was
more important than race divisions, many West Indians pre-
ferred to seek work in another country rather than face humilia-
tion for performing low-status work.

The First Wave Out

The final blow to the economies of the West Indian islands
occurred between 1880 and 1890, when several European countries started exporting beet sugar that could be grown in the

harsher European climate. The price of cane sugar plummeted and conditions in the West Indies worsened. By the turn of the 20th century, competition from beet sugar, the importation of Indian and Chinese workers, and the devastation of sugar crops by hurricanes had taken their toll. Not only were field hands out of work, but the economies of many of the islands were crippled, and skilled and professional workers were forced to take their services elsewhere. Riots occurred in Jamaica, Trinidad, British Guiana, St. Lucia, Antigua, and Barbuda between 1902 and 1920. The first major exodus of West Indians coincided with the dawn of a new century and stemmed mostly from Jamaica and Barbados, heavily populated islands that were hit hard by the fall of sugar prices.

But one of the major reasons West Indians left their homes at all was the need for workers elsewhere. The building of the Panama Canal between 1904 and 1914 drew as many as 60,000 Barbadians who saw the chance to make a quick fortune as hired hands. Between 1900 and 1920, as many as 12,000 Bahamians went to Miami to participate in the growing city's building boom. South and Central America beckoned as well, seeking workers for the Venezuelan oil fields and farmhands for Colombia, Nicaragua, Honduras, Guatemala, Costa Rica, and Brazil. The Caribbean Islands, central to all the Americas, became a gold mine for recruiting workers.

As this pattern of migration developed in the West Indies, first between islands and in small part to the United States, and later in large numbers to North, Central, and South America, West Indians grew used to the idea of moving around. Migration became a natural part of West Indian life. Twelve thousand Bahamians emigrating to Miami over two decades may not seem like a lot of immigrants compared to the hordes who were flocking to the United States during the same period, but these numbers represent an extremely large portion of the small populations on these small islands.

Once emigration became the norm among West Indians, a chain reaction occurred. When the emigrants who had traveled to other countries told their friends and kin about the prosperity that existed in their new homelands, more West Indians left in search of the same. This chain migration continues today as stories from West Indian Americans convince those still living in the Caribbean to journey to the United States. In fact, so many people have left the West Indies for the United States that everyone there knows of at least one person who has emigrated to this country.

The digging of the Panama Canal at the turn of the century. One of the first contacts West Indians had with the lure of the American dollar was during their migration to construct the canal for the United States.

Nowhere To Go

The first wave of West Indian immigration ended in the 1920s, in part due to the stock market crash of 1929 and the Great Depression that followed. But the *causes* of West Indian emigration did not end. Instead, they were worsened by the international depression. Though fewer children were born in the West Indies in the years after 1920, more survived because of improved disease control and medical advances. The population boom continued and was amplified by the many emigrants who returned from the United States because they were forced out of work by the Depression. The result was civil unrest on many of the islands. Between 1935 and 1938, labor strikes and riots took place throughout the Caribbean, particularly in Barbados, Trinidad, St. Vincent, St. Lucia, British Guiana, and Jamaica, caused mainly by the increase in population, another round of bad sugar crops, and the return of emigrants.

More than ever, West Indians needed to escape these conditions. But since the United States was no longer a willing recipient of the streams of emigrants, they headed toward Venezuela to work in the American-owned oil fields or to Curaçao (a Caribbean Island colony of the Netherlands), where the oil refineries were located.

When the Great Depression ended and World War II began, the opportunities for West Indians in the United States reopened. Americans joined the military and farm and factory jobs were left untended. Women filled many of these positions, but the U.S. government was forced to recruit workers from outside the country through the Bracero Program to keep industry

producing to meet the wartime demand. The program filled jobs
in agriculture, the railroads, the lumber industry, and in many
factories converted for war production. A majority of the workers came from Mexico *(bracero* is Spanish for laborer, and often
refers to a Mexican worker in the United States), but the U.S.
government also looked to the West Indies for recruits through
the British West Indian Temporary Alien Labor Program, a
branch of the Bracero Program, because the West Indies was
closer to the eastern United States than Mexico. The first workers came from the closer northern Caribbean islands, such as
Jamaica and the Bahamas, but pressure from other islands' governments persuaded the United States to include workers from
Barbados and British Honduras.

The Bracero Program was extended after World War II to
meet industry's needs in the prosperous 1950s, and West
Indians continued to be recruited to work. More of the West
Indian territories, such as St. Vincent and St. Lucia, sent workers. Even after Mexico's participation in the program ended in
1964, recruitment in the Caribbean continued under the H-2
Temporary Agricultural Worker Program, which still imports
workers to cut sugarcane in Florida or pick apples in Vermont.

Independence

The 1960s, 1970s, and 1980s saw many changes in the
West Indies, particularly in political control of the island govern-
ments. In 1958, Britain experimented with independence for
Antigua and Barbuda, Barbados, the Cayman Islands, Dominica,

(continued on page 18)

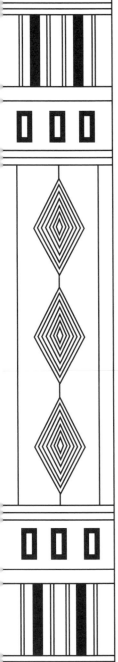

John Belazar
Green Card

John Belazar is 29 years old. He lives in Miami, Florida, and works as a waiter.

All the men in my family have been emigrants. My grandfather left St. Lucia to work on the Panama Canal. Instead of returning, he went to Belize and started his own clothing store. His brother went to Miami to work on construction, which was probably the better choice. My father spent 15 years working the oil fields in Venezuela. His brother went to Miami and stayed. My father came back to Belize.

When I was 19, I, too, decided to leave. Almost everyone I knew was unemployed. I came to Florida as a temporary agricultural worker. This is not the kind of life I wanted to live. I left the cane fields one hot and miserable day and came to Miami in search of relatives. I found my cousin Robert first. It wasn't difficult. I just looked in the phone book.

Most of my family in Miami are in business for themselves. They all help one another and other people from the community. Everyone's money together can get more done than just one person's money—that is what they say. It seems to work.

My cousin Robert was in school to train for hotel management. He said most top hotels always need high-quality waiters. He was able to get me started as a busboy in a good hotel. I didn't see myself working in a store with family. I wanted my independence. But I still had the problem that I had an agricultural visa and it was about to run out.

One of the other busboys, Ramon, was Cuban. He was born in this country as was his sister, Isabell. She was trying to work and go to secretarial school. We made an agreement. She would marry me so I would be legal and I would pay her a

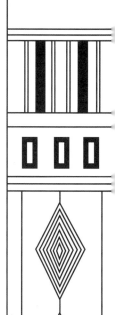

certain amount of money a month for two years. Some people think this is a terrible thing to do, but it worked out for us.

We had to prove to immigration that we were really married. We lived in a one-bedroom apartment as roommates. I got to sleep on the couch! We reported to immigration and had to show a marriage license and rent receipts. They also came to visit. I was very frightened when they came to our house. This was so important to me. The woman was nice but looked in our closet to see if our clothes were there together. She had to decide if we really were married and not just pretending. We were sitting in the front room and she was asking us questions and I started to shake. I couldn't help it. Isabell moved close to me, took my hand, and put her head on my shoulder. "Don't worry, love," she said, "it will be okay." The lady from immigration smiled at us. I think that is how I got my green card. Isabell said later that I looked so pathetic that she really did want to comfort me. God bless Isabell!

Isabell and I are still friends today. She graduated from secretarial school and has a good job with an architecture firm. We divorced, of course, and she got married for real a couple of years ago. I danced at her wedding. She's always trying to find nice women to introduce me to, but so far I like single life.

She also wants me to go to school. That is not a bad idea, but I work as a waiter at one of the best restaurants in Miami. This might not sound too impressive, but I make over $200 a night. Sometimes more. I send money to my family in Belize, who really needs it. My brother lives with me now. My sister may come soon. I have responsibilities.

Who knows what will happen when I have a family? Maybe my son will decide to move to Barbados or Belize or New York City or even Paris. We are not the kind of people to sit still when we can make a better life somewhere else.

Grenada, Jamaica, St. Kitts-Nevis, St. Lucia, and St. Vincent, by forming the West Indies Federation. The federation was to be an independent state under the British Commonwealth, totally self-governing with an allegiance to the queen of England. The West Indies was not the only area being decolonized by the British; African, Asian, and Middle Eastern colonies formed similar federations. The experiment failed because of internal strife, and the West Indies Federation dissolved in 1962. Yet Britain knew that decolonization had to occur, so it started by granting independence to Jamaica and Trinidad and Tobago in 1962.

Independence followed for most of the West Indian colonies: Barbados and Guyana in 1966; the Bahamas in 1973; Grenada in 1974; Dominica in 1978; St. Lucia and St. Vincent and the Grenadines in 1979; Antigua and Barbuda and Belize in 1981; and St. Kitts-Nevis in 1983. These countries are independent members of the Commonwealth, a voluntary association of states with a common political and constitutional base and an allegiance to the British sovereign (Guyana abandoned the Commonwealth in 1970 and Dominica does not recognize the queen as its monarch). Only Anguilla, Bermuda, the British Virgin Islands, the Cayman Islands, and Montserrat remain British colonies. Yet independence did not come easily for the West Indies. Several countries experienced political upheaval and almost all suffered periods of economic strife. Some continue to struggle with economic problems today.

Unrest in Jamaica has probably been the most prominent of the West Indian political crises. Tens of thousands of Jamaicans leave that country each year to come to the United States, despite a booming tourism industry there. A consistent population explosion keeps population density high, especially around the capital of Kingston. A socialist government, elected in 1972 and headed by Michael Norman Manley and the People's National Party (PNP), left the economy of Jamaica in a severe crisis and threatened military security. Many Jamaicans fled a political situation unfriendly to private business and the upper class--the wealthy, in particular, were the targets of violence and crime. They also left a country where skilled workers and professionals, who had trained and studied for many years, were sorely underpaid.

When the capitalism-friendly Jamaica Labour Party (JLP) took office in 1980, tourism picked up again and unemployment fell from 26 percent to 18 percent. But government services declined and prices soared, making the poor poorer. Jamaicans emigrated in substantial numbers to escape this poverty. Manley resumed power in 1989 and promised programs more moderate than his 1970s socialist plan. In 1992, Manley's deputy prime minister, Percival J. Patterson, succeeded Manley, who retired for health reasons, as prime minister. Like Manley, Patterson hopes to cure what ails the economy, but emigration has not decreased.

Since independence in 1978, Dominica has been plagued by political confusion, including the indictment and conviction on conspiracy charges of former prime minister Patrick Roland John. During the struggle for power in the late 1970s and early 1980s, general strikes and opposition demonstrations occurred, as a series of hurricanes devastated the banana industry that is central to the country's economy. Though the 1980s affluence brought an increase in tourism to Dominica, 1989's Hurricane

An American soldier and a Grenadian boy in 1983. The 1983 invasion of Grenada by the United States sent many Grenadians fleeing.

Hugo wreaked havoc on the island, crippling already slow development. The precarious state of Dominica has led many to leave
in the hopes of settling in a more economically and politically
stable country.

Guyana has been mired in severe economic problems since
1975, when falling export prices forced the government to take control of the sugar and bauxite-mining industries. There existed such
shortages that smuggling and black market sales were rampant.

St. Vincent endured massive devastation in 1979 with a
series of volcanic eruptions. The economy has begun to recover
since the 1984 elections, but unemployment at outrageous levels of 40 percent to 45 percent has not dropped, and a harsh
tropical storm in 1986 damaged the banana industry, a mainstay
of the Vincentian economy.

There is widespread unemployment in Belize, where the
average yearly income is $1,000. Grenada, the site of an
American military invasion in 1983 to overthrow communist
sympathizers, has unemployment levels that continually hover
at 30 percent. Even Barbados, which was given an excellent
credit rating by financial publications in the 1980s, and St.
Lucia, which has experienced financial growth since 1988, are
faced with rising unemployment in the 1990s. St. Lucia is particularly hard hit because current population growth is so relent-
less that the present levels will lead to a doubling of the population by 2015.

Clearly, tens of thousands of West Indians have been emigrating since the 1960s in search of better economic opportunities. If unemployment and prices are high and wages are low,
then why not look for a better place to live and work? And
knowing that the higher wages that exist in other countries will

buy more for one's family in the West Indies (especially if the wages are in strong American dollars) certainly encourages potential emigrants to pack up and leave. Throughout their economic crises, the countries of the West Indies *encouraged* emigration because it helped solve population problems, and the money sent back to relatives boosted the countries' finances. They particularly encouraged West Indians to go to the wealthy and nearby United States in hopes of an influx of American cash to jump-start the economies.

= 2 =

Why the United States?

The Influence of the Dollar

After emancipation, black West Indians went looking for work. The most logical places for them to go in the 19th century were the other islands and countries experiencing building and agricultural booms. Between 1838 and 1885, many migrating West Indians ventured to Trinidad and Tobago, acquired by Britain from Spain in 1802, and British Guiana, ceded to Britain by the Netherlands. Jamaicans, in particular, went to Panama in the 1850s to work on railroad construction. However, by the end of the 19th century, the destinations of West Indian immigrants were often ones where U.S. investment dollars were hard at work.

The digging of the Panama Canal began in 1880 under the direction of the French Inter-Oceanic Company. But the French project went bust in 1894, and the United States bought the rights to the canal and the railroad properties. Construction of the canal resumed in 1904. From 1904 to 1914, when the canal was completed, Jamaicans and Barbadians flocked to Panama at the insistence of American recruiters. As many as 60,000 Barbadians may have gone there in the ten-year period.

West Indian emigration to Panama is significant

Harlem's 135th Street business district in 1927. In the 1920s about one-fifth of Harlem's businesses were owned by West Indian Americans.

because the money used to pay workers on the canal construction was American money. U.S. dollars supported West Indian workers in other areas as well. The development of the sugar industries in Cuba and the Dominican Republic, particularly during Cuba's period of U.S. protection (1899-1902) following the Spanish-American War, was rooted in U.S. investments. Expansion of banana cultivation and railroad construction in the Yucatan, Colombia, Nicaragua, Honduras, Guatemala, and Costa Rica began with U.S. financial assistance. Between 1916 and 1929, migration to Venezuela and Curaçao brought West Indian workers to oil fields and refineries controlled by U.S. oil companies.

West Indians prospered in these other countries with the help of U.S. money. So when the Panama Canal was completed,

and West Indians went looking for more opportunities to escape the bad economic times that plagued their countries, they naturally turned to the United States. They had seen how powerful and wealthy the United States was; they had experienced the power of having American money. This country, already the destination of millions of immigrants from Europe, shone as a beacon of opportunity for West Indians.

Indeed, opportunities here were endless. Between 1891 and 1910—two decades—230,000 West Indians came to the United States. The country was growing and immigrant labor was helping to build it. Miami, a budding resort town, employed as many as 12,000 Bahamians in construction between 1900 and 1920. Harlem, a neighborhood in New York City that was formerly home to white immigrants, was becoming a haven for African Americans. It is estimated that by the 1920s, anywhere from one-tenth to one-fourth of Harlem was West Indian, comprising at least 20 percent of that area's business owners and professionals. And when World War I claimed many Americans for the military and the war services, West Indians were recruited to work in agriculture and industry left without laborers. Once here, West Indians wrote home or went back to the islands with stories about America, "the promised land." They dressed in expensive clothes and came with gifts for everyone. These elaborate displays certainly convinced more West Indians to seek their fortune in the United States, especially during the enormous prosperity of the 1920s.

Another reason West Indian emigrants chose the United States as a destination was the ease with which they could travel here. In the 19th century, new steamship lines between the Caribbean and ports on the East Coast of the United States had opened. Passage to America became inexpensive and accessible. In addition, Americans spoke English, making communication for West Indians much easier than it would be in any of the Spanish- or Portuguese-speaking countries of South America that were enjoying similar prosperity at the turn of the century. And though West Indians could always venture to England, the mother country, the United States was closer and slightly more receptive—though not for long—to black immigrants.

Even today, the nearness of this country to the West Indies is a major factor in convincing West Indian emigrants to choose the United States as their destination. Flights from the Caribbean are relatively inexpensive. Getting to the United States is easy, and more importantly, going back to visit family is just as easy. Because West Indians tend to emigrate one at a time, ties to family left back in the islands remain very strong. Being able to visit whenever possible or telephone regularly is a reason many West Indian Americans cite when asked why they chose the United States over another destination. West Indians can and do travel to other countries where, like the United States, salaries are high. They are recruited to work in the oil industry in Saudi Arabia or Kuwait, and some travel to other English-speaking countries such as Australia or New Zealand, but most come to the United States simply because it is closer. Caribbean immigrants are different from European or Asian immigrants because they consider themselves temporary visitors in the United States. Because the United States is so close, it is not viewed as a "frontier" to conquer but a place to work for a little while, even though most West Indian Americans never move back to the Caribbean.

The Professionals and Their Educations

The black professionals who came from the Caribbean had an advantage over American-born blacks. Because blacks were (and are) the majority in the West Indies, many studied to become doctors, lawyers, dentists, et cetera. The small white minority could not hope to supply enough professionals to serve the growing population, so blacks filled in the gaps. Though most of the upper class was white or mulatto (light-skinned black, of some white parentage), color did not prevent a darker-skinned black from overcoming these superficial barriers through education and achievement. Thus many West Indians strove to attain positions of influence.

Blacks in the West Indies had the benefit of English schooling, from which they were not excluded. Because education and wealth were highly valued, many West Indians studied to become professionals. But West Indian society could not afford to support so many specialists, and many emigrated to the United States in the hopes of practicing their trades in a place where they were needed. Furthermore, within a wealthy American economy, West Indian professionals could look forward to making more money in the United States than in the Caribbean.

Not every West Indian came to the United States looking for work, however. Many saw the United States as the best place to complete the education they held so dear. Though education was—and still is—important in the West Indian coun-

(continued on page 30)

Clive Johnson, Jr.
Two Cultures

Clive Johnson, Jr., is an assistant producer of news at a major television network. He lives in New York City. His father is Jamaican.

My father came to New York from Jamaica in 1955 on a tourist visa to visit his uncle Tito. At least that's what his visa said. He was 16 and wanted to study modern dance. He was lucky as well as talented. Martha Graham took him on as a student. The Queen of Modern Dance liked my father's long, graceful limbs and his quiet desire to dance.

My father's life is a fairy tale, really. He danced. He met my mother, Estelle, the daughter of Russian Jewish immigrants. She also danced with Martha Graham. They traveled all over the world. In New York, they lived in Greenwich Village, among many artists and dancers and writers. They met with very little prejudice.

In 1961, my father joined the Alvin Ailey dance company. It was an exciting time for him. Alvin Ailey's American Dance Theater was African American. The movements used by the Ailey Company were looser, and the music was more rhythmic than with Martha Graham. My father said he found joy again in dance with Alvin Ailey. It was an innovative dance company and he was there at almost the beginning.

Friends sometimes ask what it was like to grow up with a black father and a white mother. As strange as it seems, I never thought of it that way. What I did think was that my father was Jamaican and my mother was American. It wasn't until I was older and ventured out on my own that I discovered that *I* was considered an African American.

My father always thought of himself as Jamaican. Sometimes on weekends we would go to Brooklyn to visit Uncle Tito's huge family. It was almost like being in Jamaica. We ate jerk chicken and roti and everyone talked with the same accent as my

father. We talked a lot about Jamaica, where my father wanted to return when he retired.

My mother never believed he would go back. She thought he would just talk about it like so many other West Indian immigrants. But my father did just as he planned. He bought a beautiful Spanish-style house with a pool in the countryside not too far from Kingston, Jamaica. My mother went to visit once, but she always said she'd never leave her home in New York. I think that house is one of the reasons my parents divorced.

My father is very happy to be back in Jamaica. He appears on local TV often and talks about cultural topics. He's kind of a hero in his country. I visit him every year and am getting to know the island and the people well. I love the tropics, but my home is New York City.

I like producing the news. I travel almost as much as my mother and father did. Only they were making history and entertaining; I observe history and inform. I like feeling that I am a part of a vast global system. I guess that is as close to belonging as I will ever get.

I am not Jamaican. I am an American. Yet I am regarded as African American without ever having been a part of an African-American community. Most people make assumptions about my background that surprise me. They ask about growing up in the ghetto or what rap music I like. Color is still a very powerful measure for judging people.

I'm not complaining, though. I've been very lucky to be a part of different cultural experiences. My parents taught me that I could achieve whatever I choose. When I have children, I hope they can know both my father's world of Jamaica and my world.

tries, funding for schools is limited by the poor economies. Many students cannot complete their education in the Caribbean, either because the schools cost too much or the student needs to work to help support a family. In the United States, education through high school is possible because one or two parents' salaries are usually enough to support a family; children don't need to work. College educations are more accessible in American cities and counties that have community colleges, and graduate programs are often less expensive as well. Many West Indians already holding prestigious degrees look to American universities for more training and education. And affirmative action programs often help West Indians go to college, an advantage that they didn't have in their native countries. West Indians round out their educations by attending cultural activities, such as films, theater, and dance, lacking in the West Indies but widely available in the United States.

After World War II

When World War II required the establishment of the Bracero Program, West Indians jumped at the chance to take the jobs in agriculture, wartime production, railroads, and the lumber industry left vacant by Americans who had gone off to fight. Between 1942, when the program began, and 1945, when the war ended, 68,000 West Indians came to the United States under the program. They considered it a chance to leave behind more than a decade of the inescapable depression economy, during which they were not welcome in the United States.

Though the Bracero Program continued for another 19 years after the war, evolving into the H-2 Temporary Agricultural Worker Program, which still exists today, it was not until 1968 that a new wave of West Indian immigrants flocked to the shores of the United States in the hopes of staying permanently. In 1952, Congress had passed the McCarran-Walter Act, which set yearly immigration quotas (numerical limits) for colonies of another country at 100 per year. Immigration from the not-yet-independent West Indian colonies slowed to a trickle. But in 1965, Congress passed a new immigration law that had been developed by Presidents John F. Kennedy and Lyndon B. Johnson. The Immigration and Nationality Act of 1965 reversed immigration trends that had been in effect since 1882. For the first time in more than 80 years, no immigrant group was excluded from entering the United States by discriminatory quotas. Every (independent) country was afforded a yearly quota of 20,000 in the hopes that families could be reunited and all races and ethnic groups would be accepted as Americans (the Western Hemisphere was given one yearly quota of 120,000).

When the Kennedy and Johnson administrations designed the immigration bill, they assured Congress that certain nations, Jamaica and other recently independent West Indian countries among them, would not send immigrants in great numbers past the first two years the act was in effect. They could not have been more wrong. The opening up of the U.S. border released a flood of immigration from many areas, including the West Indies.

Three years earlier, Britain had passed the Commonwealth

With the
passage of an
immigration act
in 1986, tens of
thousands of
undocumented
West Indian
immigrants were
granted
amnesty. This
allowed them to
remain in the
United States
despite the fact
that they had
entered the
country illegally.

Immigrants Act of 1962, sharply cutting West Indian immigration to England by setting down strict regulations on employment certification. Few Caribbean immigrants could meet those standards. In addition, Britain was deporting (sending back to their native countries) between 1,000 and 2,000 West Indians a year. When the McCarran-Walter Act closed the door on West Indian immigration to the United States, British subjects had turned to the mother country as a destination. But now that Britain had closed its own doors and the United States was opening new ones, West Indian immigration to this country naturally blossomed again.

Three times as many West Indians came to the United States in the 1960s—half a million people—as had come in the 1950s. By the time Britain nailed the door shut in 1981 with the Nationality Act, deeming all colonial subjects as legal aliens, the flow of West Indian immigration to the United States was irreversible.

Conditions in the United States at the time the 1965 act went into effect in 1968 were ideal for West Indian immigration. The act set down a series of preference categories, in order of desirability, of the different reasons immigrants might come to this country. At the top of the list were immediate relatives of American citizens or permanent residents. They could come without any restrictions on their numbers. After that, the preference system favored skilled workers with "exceptional" or "extraordinary" abilities and more distant relatives of Americans and permanent residents, all of whom were subject to the 20,000-per-year quota. Those with the best chance of getting into the United States based on their occupation worked in professions where there were shortages in this country.

 (continued on page 36)

Charlotte Watler
A Good Education

Charlotte Watler is from Grand Cayman. She is a nurse and has lived in Boston for 20 years.

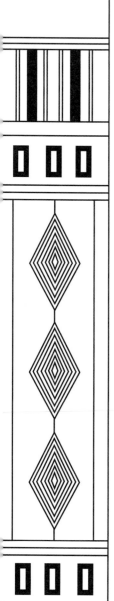

My first move as an emigrant was just a short distance to Jamaica. That's where I went to nursing school. Before we graduated, my two girlfriends and I knew that we wanted to go to the United States. They were Jamaican and had friends in Boston. After graduation, we emigrated. It was easy for nurses back then.

We had only enough money to get to Boston and stay with friends. We lived, six of us, in a one-bedroom apartment for several months. Once we found jobs, my friends and I found an apartment of our own.

That first winter in Boston was very hard for me. My sense of adventure disappeared. I was so cold. I missed my family. I would dream almost every night of the wide, uncluttered beaches of the Caymans. I thought I would save enough money and go home.

Instead, I met Phil. He came to a carnival party with the brother of one of my friends. They worked in an engineering firm together as draftsmen. Phil was half African American and half Native American. I wanted to know him immediately. He had just moved to Boston from Oklahoma City. We each thought the other was exotic.

I guess I don't need to tell you that we married that same year. I've been married to Phil almost as long as I've been in the U.S. We've had our struggles. Especially when our children were younger. There was a lot of busing going on then to integrate the Boston public school system. A lot of Irish Americans in particular didn't like that. They yelled "nigger" at our children and tried to stop the buses. I have to say that I was shocked. Although I've met with some prejudice in this country, that was the first time I had met with hatred. It wasn't new to Phil, though. He fought very hard with a parents' organization to keep our children safe and allow them a good education. Believe me, it was an education for me, too.

We try to get to Oklahoma once every two years to visit Phil's family. The kids are fascinated with the Native-American traditions of the Cherokee, my husband's mother's tribe. The year we don't go to Oklahoma, we go to the Grand Cayman. Our children are aware of their unique background.

Sometimes we don't get to make a trip. Phil went back to school and got his engineering degree, but times can be hard for engineers. He's had a few periods of unemployment. But I've always had work as a nurse. I still enjoy it, too. I've worked as a public health nurse for the past five years.

We've been lucky, all in all. Our oldest child graduates from high school this year. Our son three years after that. We talk about moving to the Caymans sometimes. Life might be slower and maybe we could relax a bit. But we have our friends here and our children have no desire to leave. So we'll probably stay.

I guess I think of myself as an American now.

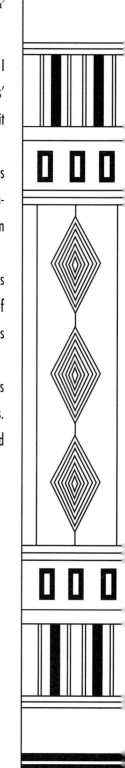

West Indians, a generally well-educated group, held an advantage in the preference system. Particularly fortunate were members of the medical profession. In the late 1960s and early 1970s, there existed a shortage of health care workers. Thousands of West Indians, mostly Jamaican women, came to the U.S. on nursing qualifications. By the early 1980s, half of West Indian professionals emigrating to the United States were nurses.

Once the current of immigrants from the Caribbean had been flowing for a few years, more West Indians came to the United States sponsored by their relatives already in the country. Once again, the process of chain migration was drawing more West Indians to emigrate to the United States. Many had already visited on vacations, admiring American lifestyles and noting how well their friends and relatives living here were faring. In fact, a chance to live in the United States was so desirable that illegal immigration from the West Indies was becoming more common.

Undocumented Immigration

Whether they come on fake passports or stay past their tourist visas, West Indians who violate U.S. immigration law by staying in the United States without a visa become undocumented immigrants. Though they are often referred to as "illegal immigrants," undocumented is more appropriate since they are some of the most law-abiding people in the U.S. They commit fewer crimes while in the U.S. than American citizens, possibly because they fear being deported.

In 1986, Congress passed an immigration act that granted amnesty to any undocumented immigrants living in the U.S. at the time. Amnesty is the government's way of overlooking the illegal entry of the undocumented immigrants and legalizing their status by giving them visas. Those who could prove that they had been living in the U.S. for five years without a break were given permanent resident status, with no questions asked. For the tens of thousands of West Indians here illegally in 1986, this amnesty was a blessing. No longer did they have to go by fake names and hide their lives from their American friends in fear that U.S. immigration officials would discover them and deport them. They could leave the country to visit relatives in the West Indies without worrying about how they would return to the

A street in the Crown Heights section of Brooklyn, New York. Changes in immigration laws since 1965 have brought more West Indian families to the United States.

United States, they could get jobs without fearing that an employer would discover a made-up social security number, and they could send for the families they had left behind in the islands.

This law created a whole new surge of immigration from the Caribbean by giving previously undocumented immigrants the permanent resident status they needed to sponsor relatives who wanted to immigrate as well. In response to this surge, Congress created a completely separate quota category, through the Immigration and Nationality Act of 1990, for the relatives of the people granted amnesty. That way, the families of the amnesty recipients could be reunited as amnesty recipients sponsored relatives who could bypass long waiting lists for immigration under other categories.

In fact, many West Indians had been immigrating to the East Coast in the 1970s and 1980s to join their families. Once the West Indians who obtained visas because of their skills settled in their new homes, they sent for their families. In those decades, parents and children of citizens and permanent residents could come without regard to quotas, at least until the 1990 act abolished the nonquota rules. Since 1990, immigrants who come here sponsored by a relative are restricted by quotas as well, though the quotas are quite large. But in the two decades after the 1965 act took effect, West Indian settlements in cities like New York, Hartford, and Miami grew considerably with the arrival of the families of West Indian Americans.

What Is Their Journey Like?

Getting a Visa

The first document an immigrant needs when traveling to America is a visa. A visa is a government document giving permission for a person to come into the country. A potential visitor to the United States applies for a visa at the American Embassy in the country from which he or she is traveling.

Foreigners who intend to live in this country permanently must apply for an immigrant visa, but those who will only be traveling temporarily can get a nonimmigrant visa. Nonimmigrant visas are issued for a specific purpose, and visitors cannot do any work other than what is allowed by the visa (for example, attend a conference, perform with a dance troupe, or not work at all if they are tourists). In addition, they cannot overstay the time limit on the visa, usually a year (less if they are tourists), without renewing it first. If a visitor overstays a nonimmigrant visa, he or she is in the U.S. illegally and can be deported. The H-2 visas given to temporary West Indian agricultural workers are nonimmigrant visas.

People trying to get any type of visa must bring to the American Consulate (a local office of the embassy) in their country birth certificates, letters from the police saying they are not criminals, and passports. They must take a physical to prove they have no contagious diseases. And those filing applications must also pay a steep fee. The fee can be as high as half the weekly salary of a factory worker in Kingston. People trying to get visas through family-sponsorship quotas must be directly related to an American citizen or immigrant with a permanent resident card, or green card.

A foreigner with an immigrant visa may apply for a resident-alien card, also known as a green card, which allows him or her to work and live in the United States permanently. However, immigrants with green cards must carry them at all times and report their current address to the Immigration and Naturalization Service (INS) once a year.

Two second-generation West Indian Americans playing in the surf on the beaches of the Bahamas during a family vacation. Few West Indian Americans become U.S. citizens because they retain such strong ties to their native countries.

After an immigrant has been in this country for five years, he or she may qualify to become a citizen. Citizenship gives one the power to vote in elections, hold certain government jobs, and bring relatives into the country more easily. In addition, all U.S. citizens, whether they were born here or not, are allowed to carry American passports, considered by some to be the most desirable in the world.

Becoming a Citizen

West Indian Americans wanting to become citizens must fulfill the same requirements as other immigrants. They must have lived in the United States for more than five years or be married to a U.S. citizen and have lived here three years (some immigrants try marrying an American citizen whom they don't know just to get citizenship, but this is illegal and is grounds for deportation). They must be over 18 and be able to speak, read, and write English at a certain level, though West Indian Americans seldom have trouble with this requirement. They must also take an oral test on basic American history, the Constitution, and the government.

Before taking the exam, immigrants fill out many forms to apply for citizenship. After the forms go to the INS, a person could wait anywhere from six months to two years before he or she is contacted to attend a preliminary hearing, where the test is administered and suitability for citizenship is determined. Those who pass have petitions for naturalization filed on their behalf.

A few months after the petition is filed, the immigrant

attends a final hearing, where he or she is sworn in as a citizen. Those getting U.S. citizenship swear an oath of loyalty to the U.S., which includes a promise to support and defend the Constitution (much like the oath the president takes). New citizens can throw away their green cards and no longer need to worry about constantly carrying a green card or notifying the INS of their whereabouts.

Surprisingly, many West Indian Americans fail to become citizens, even when they have lived in the United States most of their lives. This has always been the case, except during the Great Depression, when many West Indians took the oath of citizenship in order to qualify for government relief programs. One of the most common reasons West Indians cite for not wanting to become citizens is the fear that they will lose the right to property they still hold in their native islands—property they consider valuable and sometimes hope to return to after retirement. What they fail to realize is that most West Indian-born Americans are allowed to retain citizenship to their native countries, even if they decide to become American citizens. Most of the West Indian countries encourage this dual citizenship in the hopes that West Indian Americans will return to the Caribbean after they have made a lot of money in the United States. These countries have also made it easier for expatriates (permanent emigrants) to own land. If they move back to the West Indies after retirement, the money they will get from their U.S. pensions will be helpful to the economies of their native countries.

Another reason West Indians are reluctant to become citizens has to do with how close they remain to their native countries. Caribbean Americans, much like Mexican Americans or

Canadian Americans, visit their native countries often and retain strong ties to friends and family still there. Studies have shown that the closer an immigrant remains to people and places in his or her country of birth, the less likely it is that he or she will become an American citizen.

Where They Settled

The earliest West Indian immigrants usually came to the United States via another island or country. Because travel within the West Indies was easier than travel to North America, West Indians often tried looking for jobs in the Caribbean first. When those jobs were filled or ceased to exist, West Indians traveled to the United States, usually aboard trade ships.

After 1900, West Indian immigrants arrived by passenger steamship, docking at main ports on the East Coast in Massachusetts, New York, and Florida. With these new arrivals, West Indian communities developed in Harlem, Brooklyn, Boston, and Miami. But those taking the steamships were wealthy West Indians, who could afford to pay the fare. Most of them were members of the mulatto upper class, who came with skills and professions.

A majority of these professionals settled in New York City's Harlem. Unfortunately, race discrimination did exist in the United States, and black professionals could only find clients among other blacks. Harlem, with its huge African-American community, provided ample employment for mulatto and black West Indian professionals.

West Indian
Americans
in Brooklyn,
New York. Most
West Indian
immigrants
settle in cities,
such as
New York,
Hartford, or
Los Angeles.

Once the West Indian community in Harlem became established, more and more West Indians came to New York City because they knew they would find familiar customs there. Those already in Manhattan moved to other boroughs of New York City, establishing a small but rapidly growing community in Brooklyn. West Indians considered Brooklyn or Queens a step up in social class because they could buy homes there. Owning property was (and still is) considered by West Indians to be a symbol of achievement—to "buy house" in the 1920s meant to establish oneself socially.

Currently, as many as one million people of Caribbean descent live in New York City (most of them in Brooklyn), giving it the largest Caribbean population of any city outside the Caribbean. A great many of the West Indian Americans in Brooklyn live in the Crown Heights or Bedford-Stuyvesant neighborhoods. Jamaican, Trinidadian, Barbadian, and Vincentian influences can be seen in the food, dress, and traditions of these neighborhoods.

Aside from New York, West Indians live in tightly knit communities in several other East Coast cities. Building on the settlements they had created earlier in the century in the towns where the steamships docked, West Indians can be found throughout the eastern part of the United States. Hartford, Connecticut, has a substantial Caribbean community. Many of its West Indian-American residents chose the area to be close to other West Indians without having to endure the hustle and bustle of New York City. Today, the size of Hartford's Caribbean-American population is second only to New York's.

Specific islanders have created neighborhoods in other cities across the nation: Nevisians populate New Haven,

Connecticut; Anguillans live in Perth Amboy, New Jersey; and Trinidadians maintain a significant community in Los Angeles, California (mostly for the climate and the chance to escape familial obligations that exist for West Indians who settle in the closer East Coast cities). The state of Florida is home to the largest population of undocumented Jamaicans in the country. West Indian neighborhoods can also be found in Detroit, Chicago, Boston, Baltimore, and many other major U.S. cities.

The Women

Most of the West Indian immigrants who came to the United States before the 1965 act were men hoping to find work to support families. The jobs taken by West Indian men were often in construction and other areas involving manual labor. Recruitment in the West Indies, especially for projects like the Bracero Program, concentrated on men. However, after 1965, more women than men emigrated from the West Indies. Under the employment requirements of the 1965 act, women found they could easily get a visa to enter the country legally. They were in demand as nurses and, more importantly, as domestic workers.

Since 1965, more West Indian women than men have immigrated to the United States. It has been relatively easy for a woman to be certified as a domestic worker—a maid, housekeeper, or nanny—and qualify for a work visa. In the late 1960s and early 1970s, American mothers began going back to work, creating a need for child care and domestic help that has grown in the 1980s and 1990s.

Once here, many of these domestic workers leave their jobs after the minimum amount of time the law requires (two years). They go on to find work in their areas of expertise—the jobs they were trained for in the West Indies. Often, these women are qualified to be professionals, but knew they would have a harder time getting visas for their true occupation because a visa applicant has to show that there is no American who could fill the job at the "prevailing wage." On the other hand, many West Indian domestic workers are undocumented, taking these jobs available to legal residents only because the employers often pay in cash and don't ask for a social security number.

Married women are often joined by their husbands soon after they arrive here. However, children are often left behind in the care of a relative to avoid the cost of child care a working mother would have to pay in the United States. Most often, this relative is the maternal grandmother, who cares for the children while the parent in the United States sends back money and clothes for them. But children might also be left with friends of the family, sometimes for years at a time.

When the parents finally are able to send for their child, they may find that the toddler they left behind has grown into a teenager they don't even recognize. The parents realize they have missed all of the child's formative years. And the children often resent being whisked away from the only life they have ever known to live with parents they barely recognize in a place that is nothing like home.

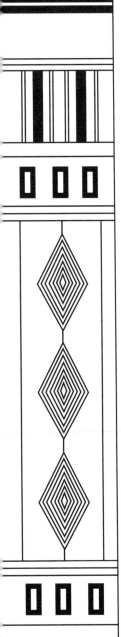

Alena Caulkins
Chasing Butterflies

Alena Caulkins is a nanny in Connecticut. She left Barbados three years ago.
She is 26 years old.

When I decided to come to the United States, I was mainly thinking of my daughter, Simone. She was five years old at the time. I looked at her one Sunday afternoon chasing butterflies and laughing and decided I wanted better for her when she grew up. Better, that is, than I had. I worked evenings washing dishes in a fancy tourist restaurant. My husband still works driving a taxi, but he pays most of his money to the taxi company and for gas.

A girlfriend of mine wrote me from Connecticut and said she was a nanny. She also said there were a lot of women in need of nannies. The job paid more than washing dishes. She said maybe I should come. She knew a woman who could arrange for me to emigrate legally if I signed a two-year contract. At first I thought I could never leave Simone. Or my husband, Marcus. That Sunday, though, after watching my daughter play, I decided I had to go. That is how I came to live with the Hansens.

I guess you could say I have a good situation. The Hansens are very nice people and I've become attached to their children. Peter is five and Francie is three and a half. We have fun together and I think they love me like they would an aunt. I have a room and bathroom that is all mine. My monthly salary is enough to save a little and send money to Simone and Marcus. Simone and Marcus live with my mother as they wait to join me.

You would think I would be happy, but I am not. I am terribly lonely. I miss Simone. I hug Peter and Francie and feed them and play with them. But they are not my children. I want to kiss my own child good-night and see her smile at me. The Hansens treat me very well, but they are not my family. I thought by now I would have my real family with me. Is my dream so unrealistic? Sometimes I feel that I am chasing butterflies, just like my young Simone.

On Sundays, I visit friends in Hartford. I don't know what I would do without my friends. We talk about our families and the islands. Sometimes we celebrate birthdays or holidays and cook special meals and dance and pretend the warm breeze is blowing—especially in the middle of January! I never knew it could be so cold.

It is strange for me living with the Hansens. Sometimes the only people I see for a week are white. Not that that's a problem, I guess. I'm just more comfortable with people who know more about me. Once one of the Hansens' friends complimented me on my English. He said I had learned to speak English very well. I was embarrassed to have to tell a lawyer that I was *raised* speaking English. You'd think he would have known.

Anyway, for now I will work and save. Soon Simone and Marcus will come to the United States. Marcus will drive a taxi here and make more money. Simone will go to good schools and study and have a chance to be a lawyer or teacher. I will give her that. Until then, I just kiss her picture every night and read Marcus's sweet letters over and over again.

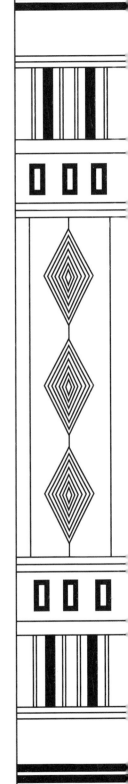

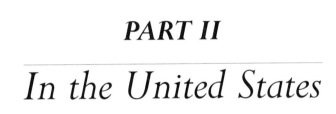

PART II

In the United States

≡ **4** ≡

Prejudices and Opportunities

Early West Indian Americans

T hough most of the West Indians who emigrated to the United States came after slavery ended in the British colonies, some very important West Indians arrived before 1838 and contributed greatly to early U.S. history.

Alexander Hamilton was born in Nevis and came to the North American colonies to get a better education. He attended King's College (now Columbia University) in New York, where he became a major advocate of American independence. He went on to become an aide to General George Washington during the Revolutionary War, establish the Bank of New York, and represent New York at the 1787 Constitutional Convention in Philadelphia. As co-author of the *Federalist Papers,* a series of essays about the Constitution, Hamilton has had a profound influence on how the Constitution has been interpreted since its ratification. In 1789, Washington, a great admirer, appointed him first secretary of the treasury, and today his face adorns the ten-dollar bill. Hamilton died in a duel with Aaron Burr, his opponent in New York politics.

John Brown Russwurm was born in Jamaica in 1799 and came to the United States to further his education. In 1826, he graduated from Bowdoin College in Maine as the first black to graduate from an American college. His success at Bowdoin opened the doors for other blacks in the 19th century to get an education at white institutions. In 1827, barely a year after he completed school, Russwurm founded the first newspaper for blacks in the United States, the *Freedom Journal.* He later emigrated to Liberia, the state in Africa set up by free blacks and former slaves, where he eventually served as governor.

A New Culture

The West Indians who immigrated in the 19th century were few in number—just 125,000 people—but they faced some obstacles when they arrived that many of their successors continued to face well into the 20th century. As immigrants to America, two things about them were different: They spoke English and almost all of them were black. The first difference worked to their advantage. But the second brought on many prejudices they had not experienced in their native countries. They were seen by whites as only "black" and not as "Jamaican," "Barbadian," or the like, yet African Americans didn't always accept them into the American black community. Thus West Indian Americans were constantly compared in performance and ability to African Americans.

West Indians discovered quickly upon their arrival that life as a black person in the United States was unlike life as a black in the Caribbean. For one thing, African Americans in the United States were a minority. Blacks were the majority throughout the West Indies. Those who came directly after emancipation still waited another 25 years—a whole generation—before slavery was abolished in their new country. But even after emancipation in the United States, African Americans were treated quite differently than West Indians had been in their home countries, though some of this different treatment made for advantages for the West Indian Americans.

Slave society in the United States was run under the assumption that African Americans were like children who needed to be constantly watched, controlled, and manipulated. Slave owners monitored every move of their slaves, hiring members of the white middle and lower classes as foremen to oversee their work. Black slaves themselves had no responsibilities.

But in the West Indies, the plantation owners didn't live year-round on their lands, and there was no substantial white middle or lower class to watch over the slaves. Instead, other blacks and mulattos were given that responsibility. Furthermore, mulattos who were born as a result of relations between a white owner and a black slave were not automatically considered slaves as they would have been in the United States. They were usually born free, and actually educated and groomed to be part of the mulatto middle class, which held positions of importance in the island governments. Some of the white plantation owners even willed their lands to their mulatto children when they left the islands.

Because West Indian slaves were given the responsibilities of farming their own plots of land, and because mulattos and blacks took positions of importance in government and industry, West Indians came away from slavery with more business sense and self-confidence. Also, because emancipation was followed by an apprenticeship period in the West Indies, not thrust upon the society in the middle of a bloody civil war as it was in the United States, West Indian ex-slaves were better prepared for their freedom.

What evolved in the West Indies was a society based on achievement and class. Whites still held the most power, with mulattos next and blacks at the bottom, but any black could easily change social position by changing economic class. There was no segregation in the schools, and unlike African Americans, West Indian blacks were not taught to defer to more powerful whites. As a result, there were fewer obstacles for West Indian blacks trying to achieve economic or political prominence than there were for American-born blacks.

When 19th-century West Indian immigrants arrived in the northern American cities, they arrived alongside an even greater number of southern African Americans. The first thing they noticed was that they were usually better educated than these Southerners, often speaking superior English. Eighty-nine percent were literate. The second thing they noticed was that this distinction meant nothing in the eyes of the white majority, who saw black as black. Unlike white immigrants of the time, who were considered "Irish," "German," or "Italian" before they were "white," West Indians were not acknowledged as "Jamaican," "Trinidadian," "Barbadian," or even "West Indian" or "British." They were seen as "black" and nothing else, regardless of ethnic origin.

Though a great number of West Indian immigrants in the 19th century were manual laborers, many had higher levels of education and were trained for skilled work. Some

A Barbadian American sits among the dry goods in his store. Many West Indian immigrants use money borrowed from rotating credit unions to fund new businesses.

were professionals. Yet most West Indian immigrants found themselves relegated to doing menial work well below their training and education. After the arrival of a substantial number of white working-class immigrants in the 19th century, blacks were rarely hired as skilled laborers, and they were certainly not allowed into labor unions that might have given them an avenue to these positions. Whites in charge of hiring were not interested in hiring black people, regardless of their education and skills. Many West Indian Americans discovered that they were excluded from being hired for the very jobs they were qualified to do.

West Indian Americans faced this racial prejudice by uniting against it. They kept their communities and their cultures separate from the American-born blacks in an effort to distinguish themselves from the southern African Americans, whom they often considered inferior. They failed to realize that the educational opportunities they had had in the West Indies were not available to African Americans in the rural South, and only on a limited basis in the North.

Rotating Credit

West Indian Americans also banded together to help one another attain financial success without depending on whites. One of the most noted achievements of early West Indian Americans was their strong representation among business owners. Some estimates note that West Indians made up 10 percent of Harlem's African-American population in 1920 but 20 percent of its business owners. West Indians were able to establish themselves so well, in what then was mostly a white-owned business area, because they formed rotating credit unions.

Rotating credit, called *box* or *partner* in Jamaica and *susu* in the eastern Caribbean, came to the United States with the West Indian immigrants, modeled on similar systems in the islands. West Indian Americans still use them today to finance various business or personal purchases. Basically, a group of friends gets together to contribute regularly to a fund—at the turn of the century, maybe 25 cents to $1.00 a week each. Every week, one of the contributors collects the amount in the fund, called a hand. The money can be used to add to business or home loans, or can be put in the bank where it will collect interest. Each member eventually gets the hand (the least-known or -trusted members get later hands), and each member is required to make every payment from beginning to end of the round.

West Indians have noted that rotating credit unions are far better than bank loans. There is no interest charged, though sometimes a member will "tip" the organizer a small fee. But more importantly, the credit unions carry very heavy social pressures with them. No one fails to make a payment because he or she would be greatly shamed. The fear of being humiliated by the gossip that would circulate after someone didn't pay keeps the money coming in. This structure is so successful that the Paragon Progressive Federal Credit Union, founded in 1939 with 12 men at 25 cents each, grew into a major banking union. By 1976, Paragon had $6 million in assets and was a financial pillar for the Bedford-Stuyvesant community in Brooklyn.

West Indian Americans used these credit unions at the

turn of the century to start businesses and escape the prejudices of white bosses and bank officers. But by opening so many businesses, they managed to alienate a lot of African Americans who resented their ambition and sometimes their arrogance. Their business savvy gave rise to a popular saying in Harlem in the 1920s: "As soon as a West Indian gets ten cents above a beggar, he opens a business."

Becoming entrepreneurs was not the only way in which early-20th-century West Indian Americans distinguished themselves. Unskilled laborers often went to trade schools to learn new skills, and those with a good educational background continued their schooling to become professionals. As many as one-third of African-American professionals in Harlem at the time were West Indian.

Two Discriminatory Immigration Acts

Though West Indian Americans were achievers, many whites still feared the growing number of black immigrants coming to the United States by the 1920s. Riding on the heels of other legislation designed to keep out nonwhite immigrants (the 1882 Chinese Exclusion Act forbade the immigration of Chinese nationals), Congress passed the National Origins Act of 1924.

The act stated that each country was to get a quota for immigration that would be 2 percent of its representation in the 1890 U.S. Census. Any country that did not send immigrants before the turn of the century (still the period of greatest immigration in U.S. history) was faced with a minimal quota. The framers of the new law were openly trying to keep the makeup of the American population as northern European as possible and keep out the Poles, Italians, and Russians who were flocking to the United States at the time. They also hoped to keep out black immigrants by stipulating that any colonies in the Western Hemisphere would be subject to the quotas of the mother country. (Independent countries in this hemisphere were not subject to quotas until the 1965 act.)

Though West Indians were then counted under a very large British quota, the law basically reduced immigration from the West Indies to a trickle because almost all the visas for Britain were granted to whites from the British Isles. Only 308 West Indian immigrants arrived in 1925 as opposed to 10,000 the year before. With the onset of the Great Depression, West Indian immigration stopped completely. In fact, many West Indians returned to the islands in the 1930s because there weren't even jobs for Americans, let alone non-Americans. Not until World War II and the Bracero Program did West Indian immigration pick up again.

During and after the war, West Indian immigration increased steadily, until as many as 50,000 West Indians came between 1941 and 1950. Fearing another onslaught of black immigrants and other "undesirables," Congress passed the McCarran-Walter Act in 1952. Separating West Indian immigration quotas from the British quota, the law assigned a yearly limit of 100 immigrants from colonial possessions, even if those colonies later became independent.

Again, Congress was blatantly trying to control the ethnic and racial makeup of the country by excluding certain immigrants. Adam Clayton Powell, Jr., an African-American congressman from New York City whose constituency included 150,000 West Indian Americans, argued (unsuccessfully) against the bill. He pointed out that the law would affect mostly black colonies in the West Indies and in Africa, and was therefore racist.

President Truman vetoed the bill when it crossed his desk, but Congress overrode his veto with a two-thirds majority. As a result, Truman put together the Presidential Commission on Immigration and Naturalization to examine the act before he left office in January of 1953. The commission returned with sharp criticism of the bill, noting that its effect on colonies in the Caribbean would severely harm U.S. relations with that area. It specifically noted that the act would be "keenly felt . . . as a racial discrimination." The West Indian legislatures in turn passed resolutions denouncing the new law.

Some Solutions . . . and Some New Discrimination

By the time that the Immigration and Nationality Act of 1965 was being formulated, Presidents Kennedy (who designed the framework of the act in 1963) and Johnson had recognized the discriminatory nature of U.S. immigration law. In an effort to end that discrimination, Kennedy proposed a bill that would give equal quotas to all countries. Ending preference in immigration by race or ethnic group, the landmark act assigned quotas of 20,000 per independent country, with unlimited immigration of relatives of American citizens or permanent residents. The Western Hemisphere had even broader quotas, with one limit of 120,000 for the whole area, until a 1976 amendment divided the countries with the 20,000-person quota.

The act proved to be a blessing for the West Indies, where the population boom was taking its toll. However, in the years since the Depression and the last great wave of West Indian immigration, the situation in the United States had changed. African Americans had won great strides in the civil rights movement, and black West Indian professionals were no longer needed to serve the black community in the United States. In

President Lyndon B. Johnson signing the Immigration Act of 1965.

addition, many of the newer West Indian immigrants were unskilled workers.

Though the 1965 act moved to eliminate racial and ethnic discrimination in immigration, it set new standards for excluding "undesirable" immigrants. With the new system of preferences and the requirement that immigrants get work certification, the 1965 law was biased toward educated, skilled workers. That is, it gave preference to the middle and upper classes. The result: a massive influx of undocumented immigrants who could not meet the standards of the employment-based preference system. One study noted that three times more West Indians came under the new law, but thousands more *undocumented* West Indians came as well.

In an attempt to stem this tide of undocumented immigration, which was not limited to Caribbean immigration, Congress passed the Immigration Reform and Control Act of 1986. This was the law that granted amnesty to undocumented workers but also made it illegal to hire immigrants without proof of their citizenship or possession of a work visa. In addition, since many of the West Indian undocumented workers were H-2 temporary agricultural workers who had overstayed their visas, the act upgraded the labor and legal protection standards for these workers.

The Immigration and Nationality Act of 1990 established yet another safeguard against illegal immigration by setting the separate quota for relatives of amnesty recipients. Congress hoped this step would reunite undocumented families once and for all, wiping the slate clean in the fight against illegal immigration.

(continued on page 66)

Chad Beaumont
Echoes of Our Fathers

Chad Beaumont is 57 years old. His parents were from the Bahamas.
He is a doctor in Nashville, Tennessee.

My father was a doctor and I never imagined I would be anything else. He was a Bahamian. This was a source of pride to him and he maintains a home in the Bahamas to this day. He is of an age that he can no longer travel, but my wife and I vacation there frequently. It is becoming a second home to us.

My father visited relatives in New York City in the 1920s. He was just out of medical school. Harlem, a district in New York City, was an exciting place to be then. He met artists and writers and politicians and intellectuals and musicians. He went to jazz clubs in the evening and sat talking for hours about politics and literature—all from a black man's perspective. He immigrated that same year.

This blossoming of the arts and racial pride was called the Harlem Renaissance. My father still regards this as one of the finest periods of his life. He met my mother during this time. She was also from the Bahamas and had immigrated with her parents. Many of the leaders of this cultural revival were from the West Indies.

When the Great Depression came in 1930, many people left in search of work. Two writers, friends of my father's, found work at Fisk University, a black college in Nashville, Tennessee. He and my mother decided to move, too, in an attempt to find a better place to raise a family. That is how I came to be born in Nashville.

My father had a private practice. He also taught at Mcharry Medical School, which was for African-American students. It was after our move to Nashville that my father and mother experienced the deepest longing for the Bahamas. They were no longer surrounded by a community made up largely of fellow immigrants or at least philosophical brothers and sisters. In this southern environment, their distinctly British speech and regal manner were thought to be snobbish. Yet my father became very committed to the students of Mcharry and my mother to her new community.

Every other summer, we spent a month in the Bahamas. This is when my father relaxed and I could see more clearly what had made this man. Those were fun, sunny days. The color of my skin was not important there. What mattered was my behavior, my education.

By the time I entered Mcharry to become a doctor, Nashville was beginning to change. I couldn't sit at a lunch counter in downtown Nashville and have lunch just because of the color of my skin. Then the lunch counter sit-ins began. All of a sudden it was dangerous and exciting. We would be served. We would be heard.

My father and mother chose this time to become American citizens. They wanted to show that they were a part of the civil rights movement, that they, too, could demand to be treated with the dignity that every man and woman deserves.

I became a doctor. I did my residency in New York City, but returned to Nashville to practice. I have a successful private practice, but like my father before me, I teach part-time at Mcharry. He said that this is something he learned in America, that it is your duty to give back to the community.

My children are the first truly American generation. They laugh sometimes at my speech, which echoes my father's. And they are angry in a way that I also find very American.

"Where is the progress, Dad?" my son asks. He has a Harvard education and teaches sociology at the University of California, Berkeley. He is immersed in African-American culture and acutely aware of inequity. My oldest daughter is an artist in New York City. She thinks my father is the luckiest man alive to have been a part of the Harlem Renaissance. My youngest daughter is in medical school. So it all continues.

I think America has been very good to us. And I think we have been good for it, too.

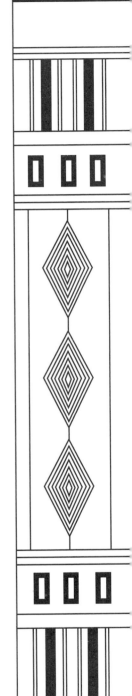

Undocumented immigration has not decreased as the result of any of these laws.

The 1990 law also set new restrictions on work certification and established for the first time a quota on immigrants who come to the United States sponsored by an immediate family member. Current law is designed to encourage the immigration of middle- and upper-class people. Those who would meet the "persons with exceptional or extraordinary abilities" requirements would be skilled or professional workers or well-known artists. Undoubtedly, they would be the wealthier people in their countries. There is also a visa preference for immigrants with a lot of money to invest in the United States—at least $500,000—or with positions of importance in foreign companies. Again, these immigrants would be wealthy. Since the West Indians most affected by recent hard times in the Caribbean have been the poorest West Indians, their chances of escaping poverty by emigrating to the United States have plummeted.

Political Involvement

One solution immigrants have always had to prejudice was political involvement to change the laws and the lawmakers supporting that prejudice. But black West Indians were at a disadvantage in the 19th century because African Americans were not allowed to vote in the United States until 1870. Even then, they were discouraged from voting by high poll taxes deliberately meant to exclude African Americans, a practice not outlawed until 1964.

Marcus Garvey, the Jamaican-American founder of the Universal Negro Improvement Association, a black separatist movement popular in the 1920s.

But early in the 20th century, West Indians took on active political roles to influence both American and WestIndian policies. They started newspapers devoted to the black cause, and they formed associations that addressed politics in the West Indies. Most of Harlem's political clubs in the 1930s were run by West Indians. They also brought from the West Indies an important activist tradition, known as street speaking.

Street speaking, also known as corner soapbox or stepladder speaking, developed in the West Indies because the white and mulatto elite controlled the press and the black majority needed to find a way to spread news. West Indians would gather to exchange information in the public square, which was usually located in front of government buildings. Inevitably the discussions turned political as news emerged from the nearby buildings.

In the United States, especially in Harlem, street speaking grew into a tradition that provided news to blacks who couldn't read the local newspapers. The topics of the street speakers were often more passionate than the newspapers' because the speakers weren't inhibited by libel laws or pressure from advertisers. Street speakers would stand on a corner, usually at an established place and time, and gather a crowd. They would talk about discrimination and encourage blacks to train for jobs. Sometimes the street speaker's role extended to helping those blacks get the training or the jobs. In his 1947 novel *Invisible Man,* Ralph Ellison depicts life in 1930s Harlem as one long succession of street gatherings led by politicians, preachers, old ladies, or Rastafarians. The hero of the novel organizes meetings and stumbles upon them in his travels up and down 125th Street. During one organizational meeting, the hero asks his partner, "How do you think we'll do?" The man responds, "It'll go big, man. All we have to do is gather them in."

Street speaking died off when World War II started. African-American politicians saw the end of the Depression and felt a new optimism for black political power. They began attracting a new following that was willing to try conventional politics to make their mark. But the street speaking movement certainly had a place in West Indian American involvement in politics.

One of the most successful street speakers and political figures in the 1920s was Marcus Garvey, a Jamaican and a leader of the Pan-African Movement. In 1916, Garvey came from Jamaica to gain support for his Universal Negro Improvement Association (UNIA), which he had formed two years earlier. Garvey advocated a black separatist philosophy—equality for blacks achieved through economic, military, and political self-sufficiency. Blacks could only become self-sufficient by separating themselves completely from white society, preferably through returning to Africa. In that interest, he formed the first all-black steamship line, the Black Star Line, established to link the black communities of the world. Garvey offered many African Americans a share in their equality through shares in Black Star sold at prices low enough to appeal to even poor blacks. He also founded *Negro World*, a critically acclaimed newspaper. At the height of the "Garvey Movement," he had as many as two to three million followers around the world.

Garvey's views were considered quite controversial among both whites and African Americans. Whites saw him as a dan-

Shirley Chisholm during her 1972 campaign for Democratic nomination for president. Congresswoman Chisholm was the first black woman to seek a major party's nomination for the office of president.

ger, but some blacks accused him of working with the Ku Klux Klan because he approved of color divisions. In 1922, Claude McKay quoted Garvey in the *Liberator:*

> "This is a white man's country. He found it, he conquered it, and we can't blame him if he wants to keep it. I am not vexed with the white man of the South for Jim-Crowing me, because I am black.
>
> "I never built any streetcars or railroads. The white man built them for his own convenience. And if I don't want to ride where he's willing to let me ride, then I'd better walk."

Garvey was convicted in 1923 of mail fraud in connection with the Black Star Line and was sent to jail. President Coolidge pardoned him in 1925, but he was deported in 1927. He died in London in 1940.

Though Garvey's movement failed, it inspired several subsequent revivals of the black separatist philosophy. Even Malcolm X, a second-generation West Indian American whose father, a Guyanese, was a follower of Garvey, advocated at one point that African Americans should be given a separate state. Malcolm X's speeches about the abilities of African Americans and the harm done to them by white American oppression continue to inspire pride and action nearly 30 years after his death. His autobiography, as told to *Roots* author Alex Haley, describes his progression from thief and pimp to dynamic speaker and antiwhite member of the Nation of Islam, to pilgrim at Mecca and believer in the equality of all races.

West Indian-American involvement in politics has continued throughout the 20th century, playing a major role in the civil rights movement and in African Americans' political participation. Many of the first African Americans to hold high political positions in New York City were West Indian Americans—one 1970 survey revealed that the highest-ranking blacks in the police department as well as all the black federal court judges in the city and several Manhattan borough presidents were all West Indian Americans. In addition, early West Indian-American activists started influential associations and aroused interest in African-American politics.

W. E. B. Du Bois, a second-generation West Indian American, earned a bachelor of arts, a master of arts, and a doctoral degree from Harvard. Editor, professor, lecturer, and prolific writer, Du Bois criticized American society's oppression of blacks throughout the early 1900s and looked to Pan-Africanism, socialism, and education as possible solutions to the problem.

Richard B. Moore, a black nationalist from Barbados and president of Harlem's Afro-American Institute in the 1920s, was one of the first to advocate the use of a term for blacks that would acknowledge their African descent.

James Farmer, a 1920s civil rights leader and one of the founders of the Congress of Racial Equality (CORE), was a second-generation West Indian American who led nonviolent protests against discrimination in public facilities. Farmer was the first to use sit-ins, standing lines, freedom rides, pilgrimages, marches, and other passive resistance techniques that became the trademarks of the civil rights movement.

Black Power got its start in the speeches of Trinidadian American Stokely Carmichael, co-founder of the Student Nonviolent Coordinating Committee (SNCC). He and the other 12 members of SNCC traveled to the Deep South in the 1960s to push for African-American voter registration. While there, the members moved in with families in poor and deprived areas to teach reading and writing and set up health clinics. In one county where no black had ever voted, SNCC registered 2,600 blacks—300 more than whites—in time for the 1968 elections. Carmichael came up with the slogan "Black Power" to discourage domination or exploitation of anyone and promote equality and equity in the power of the society.

Shirley Chisholm was brought up in Barbados, but returned to the United States, where she had been born, to become active in local politics in the Bedford-Stuyvesant section of Brooklyn. In 1969, Chisholm became the first African-American woman elected to Congress, and in 1972 she became the first African-American woman to run for a major party nomination for president.

Voluntary Associations

Not every West Indian joined the political fray, however. Some West Indian Americans living in the northern cities joined associations meant to give them a sense of community in a large place and keep them in touch with their native islands. Some of these organizations were politically active, though more often in the Caribbean than in the United States. However, membership in one of these groups did give West Indian Americans a place to exert influence, at least on a small scale, and often provided sick, hospital, and death benefits to its members.

Early immigrants joined the Masons, an international secret society, or similar organizations such as the Odd Fellows, Guiding Star of Moses, and the Foresters. The father of the black Masonic movement in the United States was a West Indian American himself. Prince Hall, born in Barbados the son of an Englishman and a mulatto woman, came to Boston at the age of 17. In 1775, Hall became one of 15 blacks initiated into the Masonic order—the first blacks in the United States to be admitted. Hall went on to fight in the Revolutionary War, urging colonists to enlist their black slaves in the army. But Hall was soon frustrated by these efforts when he realized that the war was not going to free the slaves. By 1784, Hall and his 14 black Masonic brothers chartered their own lodge, the first black Masonic lodge in America. The black lodge became a strong force in the abolition movement.

The other voluntary associations the West Indian Americans joined fell into three categories. There were those groups meant to help all West Indians get used to American society, such as the West Indian Reform Association, the West Indian Committee in America, and the Caribbean Union. Then there were the black nationalist groups such as Marcus Garvey's UNIA. The third type of organization centered around a particular island and its culture.

Benevolent associations, as they were often called, were formed to help West Indian Americans keep strong ties with their native island. Because West Indians identify themselves by the island from which they originated, these groups were a natural display of those cultural ties. The St. Vincent Benevolent Association and the Jamaican Progressive League are two examples of these culturally oriented groups. These associations concentrated on bettering the native towns and

A West Indian-American girl studying in an American school. West Indian countries can boast some of the highest literacy rates in the world, but may have inferior school systems because of failing economies.

islands of its members by sending money for clothes and school supplies or building new schools or government buildings.

Besides keeping the West Indian Americans tied closely to their home countries, these associations boosted their members' social standings back in the islands as well as boosting the standings of relatives they left behind. Voluntary associations are in a downturn these days because of strides made in black civil rights and because, in an effort to present a united front, West Indian Americans are identifying politically more with being Caribbean and African American than with being from individual countries.

In American Schools

Though voluntary associations do much to better conditions in their native countries, particularly through supporting and funding education, many West Indians look to the United States as a place where their school-age children can get a better education than they would have in the Caribbean. West Indians put great store in education, but many school facilities in the West Indies are deteriorating as the economy worsens and funds run out. Literacy rates run very high in the West Indies—as high as 99 percent in Barbados and 98 percent in Jamaica and Trinidad—because West Indians feel so strongly about the value of being educated. But schooling past the level where children learn to read and write has become more difficult in recent years in the West Indies. American schools offer the superior education West Indians would like for their children but often can't get in the Caribbean.

For some, however, the American schools prove to be a huge obstacle in West Indian Americans' education. Many children have come from rural areas of the Caribbean, where they may have missed a lot of school to help their families by working. Once in the United States, they are either placed in a grade above what they have achieved or they are held back and feel ashamed of being older than the other students. In the classroom, they can face ridicule from their classmates and even teachers because of accents so thick that they can't be understood. Some teachers don't even realize they're speaking English. Often, the student uses words or whole speech from a French-Caribbean dialect, or patois. Students who speak with heavy accents or use Caribbean words that others don't under-

West Indian-American college students at work in the Brooklyn Public Library.

stand soon stop participating in class for fear of being laughed at.

Other students can be placed at a disadvantage because their English *is* understood. Sometimes teachers or American students will assume that a West Indian speaking English must have had experiences similar to American-born black children. They will not give them the special care or attention they may need as new immigrants.

West Indian students who spent considerable time getting used to Caribbean schools before coming to the United States have another problem that plagues both parents and teachers. West Indian schools are extremely disciplined, demanding extreme quiet and respect for the teacher. Children are rarely asked to participate, and they expect punishment rather than reasoning if they do something wrong. The contrasting freedom students have in American schools tends to make West Indian students "go crazy" in the new environment. Parents of West Indian-American students complain about this lack of order, lamenting that their children lose respect for them in the United States. They resent American schools' encouragement of independence and free thinking among students. Many West Indian Americans try to avoid these conflicts between culture and American schooling by sending their children to West Indian-American-run or parochial schools, which tend to be more disciplined but cost less than other private schools in America.

West Indian-American parents in turn can be criticized by the schools and by society because of the amount of discipline they administer to their children. By American standards, the physical punishment they give might be considered child abuse, even though it would be acceptable in the Caribbean.

Sometimes teachers and school administrators intervene on behalf of the child but fail to get an understanding about West Indian customs before accusing parents of abuse. This approach can cause parents to be resentful of the school, rather than less physical with their children. Such misunderstandings among students, teachers, and parents can only harm the West Indian-American child's education in the United States.

The children aren't the only ones who can face problems in education. Many West Indian-American immigrants of college age attend local universities in an effort to further their education. But a majority of West Indian immigrants attend school while holding down full-time jobs. They end up working twice as hard to compete with American-born college students who have more time to devote to their studies.

The American Image of the West Indian

West Indians face an interesting prejudice when they come to the United States. They are usually black, but they aren't black Americans. Consequently, they are alienated from white society because they aren't white, and they are alienated from African-American society because they aren't American. They are double outsiders.

Yet over the years, West Indians have profited from attitudes Americans have toward them. West Indians in America have traditionally succeeded in white-dominated businesses, and some scholars have theorized that West Indians are given preference by Americans, particularly whites, because West

 (continued on page 82)

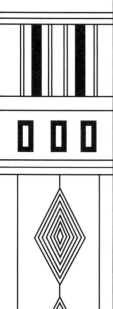

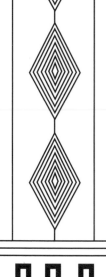

Jade Comstock
My Place in the World

Jade Comstock is from Antigua. She is 23 years old and attends the University of Florida, in Gainesville.

My family moved to Miami when I was 13 years old. I didn't want to go. I had just kissed my first boyfriend. My two younger sisters and I cried for days. We thought my parents were very cruel to take us from our friends.

And now? Now I am 23 years old and graduating from college. I think my parents were very wise and brave and I'm grateful to them. In reality, my life has been much fuller because of the move. It hasn't been easy for my parents, though. They have had to work very hard at many low-paying jobs to give us this chance. They now have a small store where they sell many goods from the West Indies. They work together, and are finally happy in this new life.

We have all learned that sometimes it is painful and difficult to get what you really want. Those first years in Miami, I thought every day about Antigua. I remembered that it was paradise. I would go to sleep at night thinking of all my favorite places, the beautiful beaches. I would have imaginary conversations with friends.

One thing that made it easier was that we knew many people from the islands. One thing that made it difficult was my speech. English is my native tongue, but I speak with a strong accent. My first teacher here wanted to put me in a special class, English as a Second Language. I had to explain to her that English was my *first* and only language. Some of the kids thought that was very funny. I didn't.

When I graduated from high school, I decided to work as a waitress and go to community college. My first year there, I discovered Jamaica Kincaid. Do you know who she is? She is a writer from Antigua, my island. She changed my life. Antigua is only 12 miles long and 9 miles wide. And she came from that tiny island and became a famous writer in the United States. I started to think that I could be somebody.

Once I discovered Jamaica Kincaid, I started reading all kinds of books, but especially contemporary writers, especially women. I decided to major in English and writing. When I came to the University of Florida in Gainesville, it was very difficult at first. I didn't have my community or family. But I had books. And because of books, I met friends who also cared about books. We weren't so much like each other except for how much we cared about reading and writing. When they smiled at my accent, I knew it was because it gave them pleasure.

My first year in Gainesville, I read a new book by Jamaica Kincaid that wasn't fiction. It was a long essay called "A Small Place." It was very angry about the situation in Antigua and it made me see my parents and their struggle in a new way. It made me look at my history as a descendant of slaves in a British-ruled colony. All of a sudden I was interested in history and politics. I started to see my place in the world and how it mattered what I did.

Last year, my family and I went back to Antigua for the first time. It was just as beautiful as I remembered. My heart was happy to see the beaches and cliffs and my old friends. But because of who I am now, the island seemed vastly different. I didn't belong there anymore. We were all very glad to have come to the United States.

I have one more year of schooling. I want to be a teacher. I want to open up books to children and show them who they are and how big the world is. And one day, I want to write a novel. I'm glad I have the memories of another place to draw on. And I'm glad I am in a country where I can write the truth.

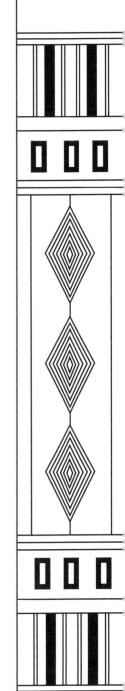

A travel agency
poster in New
York prominently
advertising
Christmas
shipping rates to
the Caribbean.
Many West Indian
Americans leave
behind close
family members
when they
emigrate.

Indians have many British characteristics. Americans' fascination with "things British" may move some Americans to give more recognition to West Indian blacks than to American-born blacks.

To their dismay, however, many West Indians also face the opposite problem when dealing with Americans. The recent surge of Jamaican immigration has brought a lot of Jamaican culture to the United States, including Rastafarianism and reggae music. Most Americans believe they can recognize a Jamaican accent when they hear one. Unfortunately for West Indian Americans who are not Jamaican, West Indian accents sound very similar. Most Americans assume upon meeting a West Indian that he or she is Jamaican, no matter which country the West Indian came from. Then they go on to assume that this "Jamaican" is a Rastafarian and is well versed in reggae music, without realizing that there are several different West Indian cultures, each distinct in its own traditions.

= 5 =

Lifestyles

The Ties That Bind

The one characteristic most West Indian Americans share is that they retain very close ties to the West Indies. So many people have left the West Indies for the United States that almost everyone there knows someone here. West Indian Americans almost surely have friends or family back in the Caribbean with whom they keep in touch. Telephone bills and travel expenses tend to be very high for West Indian Americans maintaining ties with their homelands.

One of the reasons ties are so close is the importance of the extended family in West Indian culture. Not only are mothers and fathers responsible for their children, but grandmothers and grandfathers and cousins and aunts and uncles have a hand in the raising of the children. Even if families are split up, they remain close. It is quite common for a relative, usually a grandmother, to take in the children while the mother or father moves to a place where there is work. And that mother or father returns with money and gifts for the children *and* the caretaker.

This dependence on the extended family affects West Indian immigration. Eventually, a West Indian American may

send for each close member of his or her family, sponsoring numerous family preference visas. On the other hand, he or she may never expect the family to come to the United States; instead, the immigrant lives his or her life here always planning to return to the Caribbean and rejoin the family. Though many never make it back, this attitude can prevent a West Indian from becoming an American citizen. Furthermore, West Indians hoping to return to the Caribbean may hold on to real estate and maintain bank accounts there in preparation for the return.

Constantly having a sense that they are temporary residents also leaves West Indian Americans critical of American life. They romanticize their former lives in the Caribbean,

An Antiguan-American woman at work. She may earn more than the average African-American woman.

sometimes unrealistically, and compare them to their lives in the United States. Usually, the United States can't compare, and the West Indian Americans find themselves unhappy with their new home.

Close ties with their homelands also keep West Indian Americans from "Americanizing" as much as other immigrants. Yet when they return to the West Indies for visits, they may no longer feel they are Jamaican or Bahamian or Vincentian or Barbadian. Native islanders may criticize them for becoming *too* "American." They come away with the feeling that they are neither West Indian nor American.

Remnants of British Rule

West Indians tend to be reserved with their emotions, not always expressing themselves. The American obsession with expressing oneself is not highly regarded among West Indians, who were taught at an early age to be proper. American-born children of West Indian Americans may also resent this reserved behavior and demand a level of affection they see among their American counterparts. Similarly, these same children may object to their parents' rules, which they often find to be stricter than the rules by which their friends live.

West Indians are more formal than Americans, a remnant of British influence during colonialism. A West Indian may not look someone in the eye out of respect, not out of rudeness. In conversations with business associates and even with friendly acquaintances, West Indians use the more formal "Mr.," "Mrs.," or "Miss" form of address. John Butler would be "Mr. Butler," even to someone he might have known for years.

Another remnant of British rule is the preoccupation with class that developed in the West Indies. West Indians developed their own social categories, which were based on the concept of nobility and class divisions that was prominent in Britain as the West Indies was being colonized by titled gentlemen. Though the class divisions primarily broke down according to race, the lines between classes were blurry. Because blacks were in the majority in the Caribbean, race division only supported class division, not claims of racial inferiority. A member of one class could advance to a higher class by attaining power or wealth. One way to gain power and wealth was through education— hence the stress on education in the West Indies. A position of power could be reached by securing a good job, but wealth was equated with property ownership.

West Indians associated property with economic secu- rity, freedom, and high status, because these were the things a lower-class black could get for himself if he could change classes. And if he could own property, he could change classes. In the United States, West Indian Americans will take on more than one job if necessary to be able to secure some property as soon as possible. This interest in (or strong interest in) owning property also explains the success of rotating credit, a method by which West Indian Americans often get the money for a house or business sooner than they would on their own.

In the Workplace

The average income of West Indian Americans is about 94 percent of the national average. In comparison, American-born blacks earn 62 percent of the national average. West Indian Americans own half of New York City's black-owned businesses and are well established in the taxi, real estate, publishing, advertising, banking, insurance, and retail clothing industries. But this comparison to American-born blacks is not always fair, since most immigrant groups have average incomes that are higher than native-born Americans. Compared to other immigrant and ethnic groups, West Indian Americans tend to earn less, possibly because of racial discrimination. Japanese Americans earn 132 percent of the national average and Jewish Americans earn 172 percent of that figure.

Within the West Indian-American group, women seem to be the star wage earners. Though African-American and West Indian-American men earn less on average than white men, African-American women, West Indian-American women in particular, earn more on average than white women. Women in general still earn 70 cents for every dollar men earn, but West Indian-American women are closing that gap faster than any other ethnic group. One reason this is the case may be that an African-American woman counts twice in affirmative action programs, once for being African-American and once for being a woman, and they fill a higher percentage of management positions in big companies than one would expect their percentage of the population would require. Since West Indian Americans are high wage earners among black ethnic groups, then West Indian American women will be high wage earners among black women.

One West Indian woman fighting early on for the rights of women was Mabel Keaton-Staupers. Born in Barbados in 1890, Keaton-Staupers came to the United States and studied to be a nurse. In 1941, she became the consultant nurse to the surgeon general of the United States. But her real work on behalf of African-American nurses came about during her years with the National Association of Colored Graduate Nurses, particularly between 1949 and 1951 when she served as its president. She fought hard for the integration of African-American nurses into American institutions. In 1951, Keaton-Staupers was awarded

West Indian
Americans
enjoy one
another's
company.

the Springarm Medal from the National Association for the Advancement of Colored People (NAACP) for "highest or noblest achievement by an American Negro."

Religion and Culture

West Indians come to the United States with a variety of religions, but few come as Fundamentalists or Baptists, the dominant religions among American-born blacks. Instead, the majority of West Indians are Anglican (Church of England), as in the case of Jamaicans, Vincentians, and Barbadians, or Roman Catholic, as with Trinidadians, Belizeans, and St. Lucians. But West Indians also represent some unique Caribbean religions, based on Christianity but incorporating African cultural elements. Because early slaves were prohibited from participating in white West Indian society (they were not allowed to take part in British church services or schooling), black West Indians maintained many African customs within slave society.

Afro-Christian religions combine the Christianity brought to the West by colonialists with the African religious traditions brought by slaves. This mysticism, known as shango in Trinidad and myal or obeah in Jamaica, has a basis in Christianity, but incorporates a belief in magic and spirits that enter a person's body when he or she participates in rituals.

These elements of magic and rituals are part of daily life. Invisibles haunt those who don't use all their abilities and can only be driven away with voodoo and rituals involving possession.

Some practitioners of Afro-Christian religions wear fetishes—objects that contain spirits to be called upon for casting spells.

Rastafarianism, prominent noticeably in Jamaica but spreading rapidly throughout the West Indies, has its roots in a combination of the Old Testament and 20th-century African history. In 1930, Ras ("Lord") Tafari was crowned Emperor Haile Selassie of Ethiopia, King of Kings, Lord of Lords, All Conquering Lion of Judah. Believed to be the direct descendant of King Solomon of Israel, who died 22 B.C., Haile Selassie was considered by his followers to be a god of the black race, even after he died in 1975. Rastas also believe they are the true Israelites, descendants of the black Hebrews cast out of Babylon. Through a supernatural being, Rastafarians will be lifted out of their oppression to live in a paradise on earth that reveals the glory of the black race.

Rastas are vegetarians and avoid alcohol. They also believe that their hair is a part of their spirit, so they leave it uncut and uncombed, growing it into "dreadlocks." They revere marijuana as a holy herb and a ritual offering.

At first the followers of Haile Selassie were mostly the poorer classes—the unemployed and disadvantaged. Recently, however, more educated and professional West Indians have joined the movement. Up to one million Rastafarians live in the United States, at least 80,000 of them in the New York City borough of Brooklyn alone. With a membership so large, they could have a strong influence on politics as an interest group. However, Rastas won't vote and can actually take power away from West Indian communities by lowering their representation at the polls.

(continued on page 94)

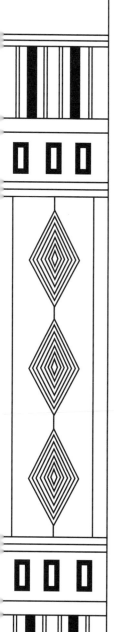

Alicia Fitzroy
Aliens

Alicia Fitzroy is 11 years old. She lives in the Bronx, New York.

I didn't want to leave my grandmama in Jamaica when we moved to New York. I was only six years old. My mother said to me, "Alicia, there's nothing here. Nothing." She worked cleaning rooms in one of the big hotels and hardly made any money. It was just her and me because my father died when I was three. I don't remember him much except that he was very tall and nice and had long, big Rasta hair. He was a Rastafarian, which is a religion. After he died, my mom went back to being a Catholic like we are now. I think she did this to forget him, but she hasn't.

The big thing that made us move, though, was a hurricane the year we left. My mom said that she couldn't take any more. We lost our house, and my grandmama moved in with my uncle. So did we until we left.

Now we live in the Bronx. Sometimes on Saturday afternoons my mom says it's just like Kingston. My school is kind of scary what with kids selling drugs and fighting sometimes. My grades are good and I study every night. My mother makes me. She says I will get a good job someday.

She works in Manhattan cleaning apartments. She makes a lot more money than in Jamaica. I go with her sometimes when she works on Saturday. Manhattan is like a completely different place than the Bronx. My mother and I pretend that we will be living in one of the nice apartments soon. I think I would like that.

On Sunday, we go to mass and then usually visit our cousins. We don't talk about mass because my cousins are Rastafarians like my father was. They are his relatives. Lucy is my age but goes to a different school. Her grades are not so great. Her

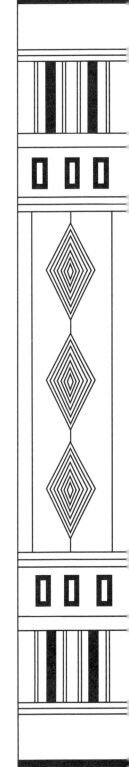

mother is not as strict as mine. She gets to go out at night with friends if she comes home early. I don't.

We mostly know people from the islands. I think that's because we are undocumented immigrants. That sounds better than illegal aliens, which makes me think of spaceships. We came here on nonimmigrant visas and just stayed. I guess we'll just keep doing this as long as we can. Mother says when I'm out of high school she will go back to Jamaica. By then, I can probably find a way to stay. I don't know if I want to yet.

My best friend at school, Josephina, is from Puerto Rico. She's legal. She's teaching me some Spanish. She says I should stay and we'll move to Manhattan and get good jobs. Who knows? I feel very out of place when I go to Manhattan. Maybe when I grow up and learn to get all my grammar straight and have good clothes, I might move there. Josephina and I would have a very good time, I'm sure.

My mother's new boyfriend was born in Brooklyn. That means if she marries him, we'll be Americans. Maybe. It's hard to know how the government works.

So for now, we both just do the best we can. We also see a lot of good movies.

These days, cultural differences between West Indians and Americans have less to do with the differences between Western and African traditions and more to do with the differences between city and rural life. Most West Indian Americans live in urban areas but originally came from rural parts of the Caribbean. There, West Indians could expect a neighbor to keep an eye out for their children or bring them something from the market. Those who did live in cities in the Caribbean became accustomed to urban centers half the size of any large city in the United States. Even Kingston, one of the largest Caribbean cities, has only 104,000 inhabitants!

Consequently, West Indians feel quite a bit of culture shock when they arrive in U.S. megacities like New York, where the population exceeds ten million, where neighbors usually keep to themselves, and where people are, more often than not, rather unfriendly. They deliberately gravitate toward the areas of these cities already inhabited by other West Indians to avoid a severe change in lifestyle. Sometimes misinterpreted by Americans to be snobbishness, this exclusivity is really a defense mechanism against cultural changes West Indians face living among Americans.

Arts and Leisure

West Indian Americans have contributed much to the arts of the United States, bringing with them traditions and styles formed in their native Caribbean. Literature, sports, music, and food in the United States all have been influenced by the presence of West Indians in this country.

One of the earlier, but still most influential, contributions of black West Indian Americans to American arts occurred in the 1920s. A period of great achievement in literature, music, and the visual arts blossomed around the time of World War I. African Americans who had joined the military during the war to prove their patriotism found that racism was much less prevalent in Europe than in America. These veterans returned to the United States with a new voice and an attitude of racial pride that spurred a period of outstanding literary achievement among African Americans. Centered in New York City's Harlem, this boom of cultural creativity was known as the Harlem Renaissance. For the first time, African-American writers expressed themselves in their own voices rather than imitating white novelists or writing "simple" works in a quaint black dialect. Harlem soon became a cultural mecca for both blacks and whites looking to take in the unique black culture in Harlem's speakeasies and jazz clubs.

One leader of the Harlem Renaissance was James Weldon Johnson, a second-generation Bahamian American. Educated at Atlanta University, Johnson became a lawyer, editor, and educator. In 1912, he wrote *Autobiography of an Ex-Coloured Man,* a novel about a black man so light-skinned that he could "pass" for white, a theme that would turn up over and over in black literature. The hero of the novel joins white society to further his musical career but finds success at this price to be hollow. The novel was a precursor to much of Harlem Renaissance writing that treated African-American subjects seriously instead of stereotyping them. Johnson himself became a mentor to many Harlem Renaissance writers.

Jamaican-born Claude McKay was another prominent West

In the 1920s Harlem was the center of the Harlem Renaissance, one of the richest periods of cultural creativity in African-American history.

Indian American involved in the Harlem Renaissance. An editor
for two radical magazines, the *Liberator* and the *Messenger,*
McKay wrote poetry, in a West Indian dialect, that attacked
racism full force. He also authored three influential novels in
the 1920s. Though McKay emigrated to Europe in 1934, his
works continued to influence African-American writers.

W. A. Domingo, also a Jamaican by birth, encouraged much
of the Harlem Renaissance when he defined the "New Negro" in
a 1920 issue of the *Messenger.* Domingo wrote that the New
Negro insisted on "absolute and unequivocal social equality," an
idea that flew in the face of the previously accepted notion that
African Americans could educate themselves and move up the
social ladder but would always have to occupy a social position
lower than that of whites.

Eric Walrond's essay "On Being Black" was published in
1925 in the *New Republic* and drew much attention. Walrond, a
Guyanese American essayist, short-story writer, and editor of
the *Negro World,* was yet another intellectual prominent in the
Harlem Renaissance.

The Harlem Renaissance ended when the Great Depression
began and the writers and artists were forced to scatter looking
for work. However, the intellectual attitudes and the literary and
artistic works produced during this period have influenced and
continue to influence many African-American writers, intellectuals, and artists. One notable contemporary writer is Antiguan
American Jamaica Kincaid, whose books include *A Small Place,*
Annie John, and *Lucy.* They are all based on her experiences
growing up in Antigua and emigrating to the United States.

The 20th century has also witnessed the emergence of a

One of the
most celebrated
black actors
in the world,
Sidney Poitier,
is a second-
generation
Bahamian
American.

number of prominent African-American entertainers, many of whom are West Indian. Harry Belafonte is a second-generation Jamaican-American singer and actor, raised in Jamaica. He popularized Caribbean music in the United States in the 1950s and was associated in the 1960s with civil rights and other African-American causes. Geoffrey Holder, born in Trinidad, has gained fame in the entertainment industry as a dancer, actor (*Live and Let Die, Doctor Doolittle*), choreographer, director (*The Wiz*, for which he won a Tony Award), costume designer, and writer. Sidney Poitier, one of the most famous African-American actors, is also a second-generation Bahamian American who was raised with his family in the Bahamas. The first African American to win an Academy Award for Best Actor (for *Lilies of the Field* in 1964), Poitier redefined the image of the African American in film. His roles in such movies as *Blackboard Jungle, Guess Who's Coming to Dinner*, and *The Defiant Ones* had strong box office appeal while depicting African Americans as intelligent and graceful, an image distinctly missing from most earlier films.

West Indian Americans come to the United States with leisure activities they have learned as British subjects. One example is their devotion to the sport of cricket, a game similar to baseball, which is the national pastime of Great Britain. The New York Cricket League was formed in 1919 and has grown to overtake several fields in Van Cortlandt Park every Saturday and Sunday between May and September. In other areas of high West Indian-American concentration, similar cricket leagues are forming. Often, the American teams made up of West Indian Americans are the best of the world amateur teams. Of course, cricket isn't the only sport West Indian Americans play well. The first black to win the world welterweight boxing title (in

1901) was Joe Walcott, a Barbadian. And one of the greatest basketball players of our time, New York Knicks' Patrick Ewing, was born in Jamaica where he lived until he was 12.

Music from the West Indies has certainly not escaped the journey to the United States. Different musical styles from different areas of the West Indies have influenced American pop and rock music. Reggae, ska, limbo, soca, calypso, steel band, and dancehall music are all forms of West Indian music that are present in American music today. Contrary to the belief of many Americans, reggae is not the only music in the West Indies. Each island in the Caribbean has developed a unique style of music, though calypso and reggae have spread among the islands in popularity.

Calypso, which has its roots in Trinidad and Antigua, had quite a stretch of popularity in the 1950s, when Caribbean and Latin music was influencing dance steps among teens. Harry Belafonte and other Caribbean performers helped popularize this craze. Soca, a modernized, electrified combination of calypso and soul music *(soca* is a combination of soul and calypso), is gaining fame as West Indian Americans introduce it to American music fans. The soca beat, now popular in Grenada, Barbados, Montserrat, and Jamaica, forms the base of many modern pop songs in the United States.

The most recognizable and most popular of Caribbean music styles to come to the United States is reggae, music with a loping, hypnotic rhythm made popular here by Jamaicans such as Bob Marley, Jimmy Cliff, and Peter Tosh. Originally associated by Americans with Jamaican Rastafarianism, reggae has influenced many American rock musicians spanning a wide array of styles. Recently, reggae has meshed with hip-hop to

Jamaican-American basketball legend Patrick Ewing moved from the Caribbean to the United States when he was 12 years old. Drafted to the NBA in 1985, he has since become one of the best players in the association.

create a new, baseline-heavy form of reggae known as dancehall. Popular in the United States through artists like Shabba Ranks, dancehall is invading clubs throughout the country.

West Indian food has become very popular in the United States in recent years, and restaurants specializing in Caribbean cuisine can be found in areas where West Indian-American communities thrive. Jerk chicken, a spicy barbecued dish, has gained popularity as Jamaicans have opened jerk restaurants and sold the sauce separately in local markets. Roti, a breadlike pastry filled with goat or chicken, is another popular West Indian food finding its way into American tastes. Other West Indian food influences have become mainstays in American cuisine, including curry(brought to the Caribbean by East Indian laborers), rum (popular in tropical summer drinks), and many unique fruits and vegetables, such as coconuts, bananas, and plantains.

As Americans become more aware of their cultural and ethnic roots, a trend that became popular in the 1970s, the influences of West Indian society have been magnified. It is fashionable in the United States to wear traditional clothing from another nation, enjoy ethnically diverse foods, and incorporate musical traditions from other cultures into American songs. Since this resurgence of ethnicity, West Indian Americans have watched their traditions and cultures gain enormous popularity among non-West Indians in the United States.

Celebrations

West Indians have several elaborate festival and holiday traditions, many of which they have brought with them to the

A West Indian restaurant in New York City. Caribbean food, first introduced by immigrants, is gaining popularity in the United States.

United States and incorporated into American life. Early West Indian Americans celebrated the Harvest Festival, when they brought their best produce to the local church to be distributed among the poor. West Indians in Harlem in the 1930s gathered at St. Cyprian's each October to decorate the church for Harvest Sunday and participate in the street fair that soon grew out of the Festival. Other early West Indian Americans threw parties to honor the British royal coronations and birthdays. Weddings and funerals (which are considered celebrations of life rather than mournings of death) are observed with up to a week of celebrations and parties surrounding each.

Trinidadians have brought their most celebrated festival, Carnival, to the United States. The month before Lent, the fasting period in many religions leading up to Easter, Trinidadians

(continued on page 106)

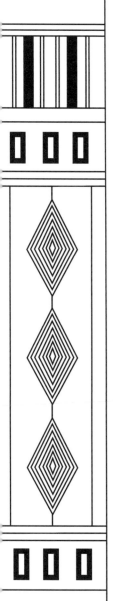

Java Kinte
The Ritual of Music

Java Kinte is from Trinidad. He has lived in Los Angeles, California, for 11 years and is 30 years old. He is a professional percussionist.

Java Kinte is not my real name. Hey, I'm in the music business! Believe me, you've got to be remembered in a town with a short attention span.

Why did I come to LA? Music. I've been playing percussion since I could walk. No lie. My dad had a cousin who played, and from the time I heard him it's what I wanted to do. He played pan, which is a drum made from steel oil barrels. That probably sounds funny to you, but it's very big in Trinidad. My cousin even plays with the symphony. But I wanted to play all the percussive instruments. And I do. My dad wasn't too thrilled with my career choice. He's an accountant. Need I say more?

I was playing in Trinidad but listening to music from all over. I got this gig with a band in St. Thomas back in 1980. While I was there, I met a drummer from Los Angeles. He said he could get me a few months of work in LA, playing sessions on two albums he was producing. He did. I couldn't believe it. I got a three-month work permit. When my permit ran out, I just stayed.

No, it's not hard staying in the U.S. as an illegal if you watch your step. I did. I was desperate to stay. Musicians from all over the world come to Los Angeles. I was in heaven. I still am. I can really play and people here know it. I tell them I'm possessed by spirits! I'm only half kidding. In Trinidad, there are certain rituals performed in a religion called shango, and they say when you do it right, spirits enter you. It's this mystic thing. Well, my music is my ritual. I think the spirits come to me and I can play better than even I ever imagined.

I'm even legal now. Sometimes things work out without even having to try very

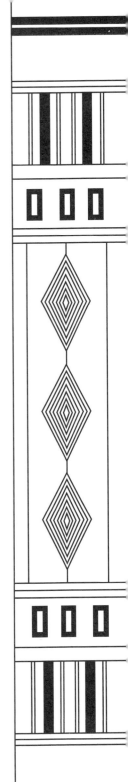

hard. In 1986, they declared amnesty for all undocumented immigrants who could prove they had lived in the United States for five years. I just made it. Let me tell you, there was a lot of paperwork. But it was worth it. I'm here to stay for sure now.

One of the best things going for me right now is this new band I'm in. We play a mixture of music. I guess you could call it world music if you want an easy tag. We've got a diverse mix of people, too. Two of the guys are African-American. James plays sax. He's from Oakland, California. Anthony plays keyboard and he's from Alabama. People lump us together because we're black, but you can't imagine three people with more dissimilar backgrounds. Actually, Anthony is almost more out of place than me here even though he's an American. He comes from a small town in rural Alabama. LA is pretty far-out to him. I come from Port-of-Spain in Trinidad, which is a big city with everything happening at once. Everyone I meet thinks I'm from Jamaica! But it's cool. What matters is we're making some music.

People complain about LA a lot, but except for the smog I wouldn't want to live anywhere else. In one week, I can hear rap, reggae, rock and roll, ska, and even Sufi music. Plus, it looks like we might get a record deal. Do I sound LA or what? It's just talk right now, but doors are opening. I can feel it. Would this have happened in Trinidad?

I go back to Trinidad almost once a year now that I'm legal. It's true that I miss it sometimes, especially my family. My only family in LA are my friends. I think about Trinidad and how it sounds and how even the smells are different. And you've never seen anything like this bird, the scarlet ibis. It's big and bright red. Dozens of them land in mango trees and it's quite a sight. But I think everybody misses the place where they spent their younger years. For me, LA is the place to be.

By the way, Trinidad is off the coast of Venezuela. I swear, peoples' geography here is funny sometimes. Trinidad is not off the coast of Florida or Africa. I've heard it all.

Trinidad is all right. Absolutely. You should visit sometime.

revel with parades, pageants, and costume contests, much like the Mardi Gras celebrations in New Orleans, Louisiana. This tradition has its roots in the Yoruban culture of western Africa, brought to the Caribbean by slaves and mixed with Spanish (the original colonists in Trinidad) Christian celebrations to create the unique Carnival atmosphere. Trinidadian Americans, when they can't get back to Trinidad for Carnival as most do, re-create the festival atmosphere in their own American neighborhoods.

One celebration West Indian Americans didn't bring directly with them from the Caribbean actually originated in New York City, the area with the largest concentration of Caribbean Americans. The West Indian Day Parade has been held on Labor Day in New York since 1969. Called *mass* or *mas* (probably short for *masquerade* or for an African word meaning "festival" or "celebration"), the parade and the surrounding festival are a grand celebration of the many cultures of West Indians. The festival incorporates foods, costumes, music, and dancing from each island, and owes much to the Carnival traditions of the Trinidadians, who most often organize the parade. Calypso, steel band, reggae, soca, merengue, and dancehall music fill the air and blend with the smell of jerk chicken and goat roti.

West Indian Americans and indeed native West Indians consider the New York parade to be the most magnificent of West Indian celebrations. People come from all over the world to participate—from across the United States, the Caribbean, even Africa. The parade has grown to enormous proportions, attracting as many as one million people in recent years. The costumes are so elaborate that they can take up to a year to make. The parade also draws huge sponsors such as IBM,

Pepsi, and American Airlines.

The West Indian Day Parade is the best place to learn about West Indian-American life. A warm celebration of camaraderie and cultural diversity, the parade and the festival are the stage where all the achievements and traditions of West Indians in America are exhibited for the world to admire and applaud.

For Further Reading

Anthony, Suzanne. *The West Indies.* New York: Chelsea House Publishers, 1989.

Du Bois, W. E. B. *The Souls of Black Folk.* New York: Fawcett Publishing, 1927.

Ellison, Ralph. *Invisible Man.* New York: Random House, 1947.

Ferguson, Ira Lunan. *Fantastic Experiences of a Half-blind and His Interracial Marriage: An Autobiography.* San Francisco: Lunan-Ferguson Library, 1982.

Haley, Alex. *The Autobiography of Malcolm X.* New York: Grove Press, 1965.

Johnson, James Weldon. *Autobiography of an Ex-Coloured Man.* New York: Knopf, 1912.

Kincaid, Jamaica. *Annie John.* New York: Plume Books, 1985.

Klevan, Miriam. *The West Indian Americans.* New York: Chelsea House, 1990.

Marshall, Paule. *Brown Girl, Brownstones.* New York: Feminist Press, 1981.

Prescod-Roberts, Margaret. *Black Women: Bringing It All Back Home.* Bristol, England: Falling Wall Press, 1980.

Reid, Ira. *The Negro Immigrant.* New York: AMS Press, 1968.

Time, July 7, 1985. Issue devoted entirely to immigrants.

Two Hundred Years of West Indian-American Contributions. Brooklyn: Herman Hall Associates, 1976.

Wilkinson, Alec. "Big Sugar." *The New Yorker,* July 24, 1989, p. 42.

Index